I COMMAND YOU TO FIGHT

//

When Giving
Up is Not
an Option

DR. SHERRY GAITHER

I Command You to Fight: When Giving Up Is Not an Option
by Dr. Sherry Gaither

copyright ©2018
ISBN: 978-1-943294-73-2

cover design by Martijn van Tilborgh

I Command You to Fight is available in Amazon Kindle, Barnes & Noble Nook and Apple iBooks.

CONTENTS

ACKNOWLEDGEMENTS

I AM SO GRATEFUL FOR THE OPPORTUNITY to do the work that I am called to—provoking individuals to live a victorious and purpose driven life. This is divine assignment in life, one that I could not do alone.

To my family: my husband, my children, my parents, my brothers and sisters, and my covenant friends, thank you for believing in me. I am so blessed to have your love and never-ending support. I love you with all my heart.

To my Stronghold Christian Church Family, thank you for your prayers and encouragement over the years. I am blessed to co-pastor and serve the greatest church in the world.

To the victorious women, who allowed me to share their powerful testimonies, I am truly grateful.

To my Lord, who is always above, beneath, behind, before, and in me, thank you for the empowering presence of the Holy Spirit.

To these, and for other unnamed, I am grateful,

—*Dr. Sherry Gaither*

CHAPTER I

INTRODUCTION

I was born to fight—for the first time I have something to fight for.—Kylo Ren, *Star Wars: The Last Jedi* (2017)

L IFE IS NOT A PLAYGROUND. It's a battlefield, and we are in a battle right now. The Apostle Paul makes it clear that we are in a spiritual struggle that is beyond flesh and blood (Eph. 6:12). Your victory depends on: (a) your understanding of the nature of the battle, (b) your ability to rely on God's power, (c) your commitment to operate according to spiritual principles, and (d) your obedience to follow God's instruction.

FIGHT ACCORDING TO THE PLAN

The Book of Deuteronomy is considered the second telling of the Israelites' flight from slavery in Egypt, through the wilderness journey. The book consists of three sermons delivered to the Israelites by Moses shortly before they enter the Promised Land. The first sermon recounts the forty years of wilderness wanderings, which had led to that moment; the second reminds the Israelites of their commitment to God; and the third warned Israel of the importance of repentance.

Prophetically, Deuteronomy talks about the future and what God will be doing in their midst. A new generation had been born. Moses ultimately dies and Joshua is chosen to lead the people. But the first message in the book is a historical summary of how God delivered the nation for His purposes.

These are the words which Moses spoke to all Israel on this side of the Jordan in the wilderness, in the plain ... It is <u>eleven</u> days' journey from Horeb by way of Mount Seir to Kadesh Barnea. Now it came to pass in the <u>fortieth year</u>, in the eleventh month, on the first day of the month, that Moses spoke to the children of Israel according to all that the Lord had given him as commandments to them, after he had killed Sihon king of the Amorites ... On this side of the Jordan in the land of Moab, Moses began to explain this law, saying, "The Lord our God spoke to us in Horeb, saying: 'You have dwelt long enough at this mountain. Turn and take your journey ... <u>See, I have set the land before you; go in and possess the land</u> which the Lord swore to your fathers—to Abraham, Isaac, and Jacob—to give to them and their descendants after them.'" (Deut. 1:1-8 NKJV)

God promised to keep the covenant He had made with Abraham (Gen. 13:14-18; Exod. 3:8). God agreed to give Israel victory over their enemies, if they would follow His orders and obey His plan. Kadesh-Barnea was the entryway into the Promised Land, but Israel walked by sight and not by faith; therefore, they failed to enter the land because of fear and unbelief. Moses challenged the people to "see" what God had already done and now it was time to possess it.

There's a difference between unbelief and doubt. Unbelief is a matter of the will; it causes people to rebel against God. Doubt, however, is a matter of the heart and the emotions and causes people to waver between fear and faith. At Kadesh, God decreed that the nation would wander for forty years, until all the people twenty years and older had died. Then He would take the new generation into the land and they would conquer the enemy and claim their inheritance.

THIS IS NOT YOUR FIGHT

In the second chapter of Deuteronomy, God guided His people through other people's land, without confrontation. Picture yourself ready for battle and anxiously waiting for the signal to attack. The message from God, according to your leader, is: Don't fight. Maintain a position of peace.

And command the people, saying, "You are about to pass through the territory of your brethren, the descendants of Esau, who live in Seir; and they will be afraid of you. Therefore watch yourselves carefully. Do not meddle with them, for I will not give you any of their land, no, not so much as one footstep, because I have given Mount Seir to Esau as a possession." (Deut. 2:4-5 NKJV)

The Edomites were descended from Jacob's brother, Esau, and Moses was commanded by God not to declare war on the people of Edom and try to take their land. God spared the Moabites and Ammonites and commanded Joshua not to fight them, because they were the descendants of Lot, the nephew of Abraham (Gen. 19:30-38).

Then the Lord said to me, "Do not harass Moab, nor contend with them in battle, for I will not give you any of their land as a possession." (Deut. 2:9)

Wilderness wandering was coming to an end, and Israel was looking forward to defeating their enemies and claiming their land, but the key to their victories was knowing whom to fight and which battles were God ordained. What does that mean to you and me? I need you to realize that God has not called you to fight every conflict, battle, and opposition that comes your way. You've heard the saying, "pick your battles." It refers to a military strategy in which the troops are spread out and fighting a war simultaneously on more than one front. The best way to ensure victory is to mobilize the forces at a strategic point and determine what enemy to fight.

Here's an example. You are financially at your lowest point because you are between jobs. You have diabetes and no insurance and your son may not be able to go back to college, because he doesn't qualify for financial aid. You are fighting on multiple levels, with no victory in sight. What is God telling you to do?

And when you come near the people of Ammon, do not harass them or meddle with them, for I will not give you any of the land of the people of Ammon as a possession. (Deut. 2:19)

IT'S TIME TO FIGHT

God would tell Joshua which city or people to attack; He would assure them of victory; and He would go with them to help them win the battle. The two powerful kings, Sihon and Og lived in the region of the Amorites on the east side of the Jordan. They were positioned to fight Israel. Since the Lord had determined to destroy them and their people, He gave Joshua specific instructions to follow. All the children of Israel had to do was obey God's orders, trust His promises, and courageously confront the enemy.

"Rise, take your journey, and cross over the River Arnon. Look, I have given into your hand Sihon the Amorite, king of Heshbon, and his land. <u>Begin to possess it, and engage him in battle</u>. This day I will begin to put the dread and fear of you upon the nations under the whole heaven, who shall hear the report of you, and shall tremble and be in anguish because of you." (Deut. 2:24-25 NKJV)

STICK TO THE PLAN

"And I sent messengers from the Wilderness of Kedemoth to Sihon king of Heshbon, with words of peace, saying, 'Let me pass through your land; I will keep strictly to the road, and I will turn neither to the right nor to the left. You shall

sell me food for money, that I may eat, and give me water for money, that I may drink; only let me pass through on foot' ... But Sihon king of Heshbon would not let us pass through, for the Lord your God hardened his spirit and made his heart obstinate, that He might deliver him into your hand, as it is this day." (Deut. 2:26-30 NKJV)

What was the plan? The strategy was to get in position, cross the river, begin possessing the land, and start a war with the enemy. King Or, one of the remnants of the giants, was very strong, and intimidating. His army was massive and very powerful. He commanded sixty fortified cites and un-walled towns. King Or knew that King Sihon had been killed, but he was audacious and he trusted in his own strength and attacked Israel.

"Then we turned and went up the road to Bashan; and Og king of Bashan came out against us, he and all his people, to battle at Edrei. And the Lord said to me, 'Do not fear him, for I have delivered him and all his people and his land into your hand; you shall do to him as you did to Sihon king of the Amorites, who dwelt at Heshbon.'" (Deut. 3:1-2 NKJV)

To possess means to own, to break through, to enlarge, and to increase. There are times when you are going to have to fight to get what belongs to you, to keep what belongs to you, and to get back what was taken from you.

Life is about choices and there are consequences for every decision. You have the choice to be either a victim or to be victorious. You must decide whether you will be in bondage to the past, paralyzed by the present, and pessimistic about your future. *I Command You to Fight* will challenge you to break free from the tormenting thoughts of: what should have been, could have been, or might have been. Right now your heart should be racing and something on the inside of you should be leaping, because you realize that God has more for you than always going through and never coming out "more than a conqueror."

Let me unpack that statement. If your doctor writes you a prescription and informs you that you will have to take "blank" (you fill in the "blank") for the rest of your life—something in you should rise up and say, "The devil is a liar." *I Command You to Fight* will provoke you to flex your spiritual muscles and remember who you are and more than that, *whose* you are. You can't afford to take a passive position and pop pills until Jesus comes. After you bombard the doctor with a lot of questions, after the enemy begins to play with your mind, after the emotional roller coaster and the tears— you declare, "By Your stripes I am healed." You command your body to line up with the Word of God, and allow the Holy Spirit to strengthen you in your inner man. Every time you take the medicine (yes, take the medicine), you declare the Word and come against the side effects of the medicine. He is the Great Physician and by His stripes, you are healed.

I Command You to Fight is a must-read for anyone who understands purpose and destiny. Jeremiah 29:11 declares, "'For I know the plans I have for you,' declares the Lord, 'plans to prosper you and not to harm you, plans to give you hope and a future'" (NIV). You must fight for your destiny because Satan also knows that God has a purpose for your "dash." The dash between your birth certificate and your death certificate is your life. You will not hear, "Well done good and faithful servant" (Matt. 25:23) for sucking up air, coasting through life, doing your own thing, or living under the circumstances.

You will have to fight to fulfill your Kingdom assignment. The enemy didn't back down when you acknowledged Jesus as your Lord and Savior. (Just in case you forgot—that is how you got saved.) If Satan could not keep you from getting saved, his goal is to spend the rest of your life keeping you from abundant life. Satan is the accuser of believers (Rev. 12:10) and he goes before God and pronounces judgment against you by saying, "He may be saved, but he keeps doing (blank), so you can't use him," or "She can't get over her issues—she'll never be the instrument for someone else's deliverance." Satan reminds God that you may be saved, but your challenged lifestyle is keeping you from accomplishing your purpose (Jer. 1:5). He accuses you daily for not living a life of holiness (Rev. 12:10).

Life is a hard fight, a struggle, a wrestling with the principle of evil, hand to hand, foot to foot. Every inch of the way is disputed. —Florence Nightingale

I Command You to Fight reveals the nature of spiritual warfare: God and His truth against Satan and his lies. With the battle lines drawn, Satan and his army of demons stand prepared to challenge God's plan for your life. The Bible clearly defines our position as soldiers in the Kingdom. We are commanded to resist the devil, endure hardship, fight the good fight of faith, and stand firmly in the midst of the battle (James 4:7; 1 Pet. 5:8-9; 2 Tim. 2:3-4). When Satan fell, every day became an evil day, but that is not an excuse for us to straddle the fence, lower the standard, or live defeated lives (Eph. 6:13). When you are grounded and rooted in God's Word, you are able to stand firm. If you fall, you get back up, get your second wind, and come out fighting. Your adversary, the devil, is counting on you to grow weary, faint, and concede defeat.

Be sober, be vigilant; because your adversary the devil walks about like a roaring lion, seeking whom he may devour. Resist him, steadfast in the faith. (1 Pet. 5:8-9 NKJV)

I Command You to Fight is not for the fainthearted or the wimpy anemic believer. This book is for warriors, who are ready to pursue and take back what has been stolen, blocked, and delayed. The Commander and Chief has secured your victory. All through the Book of Revelation, you will read these words: "to him that overcomes." To overcome means to triumph, to stay in the game, to be persistent, to finish strong. But again I say, it will not happen without a fight.

Yet in all these things we are more than conquerors through Him who loved us. (Rom. 8:37 NKJV)

I COMMAND YOU TO FIGHT

I Command You to Fight is for individuals who refuse to lie down and die, abandon their assignment, run from their calling, and abort their dreams. The greater the call, the greater the warfare. The greater your faith, the greater the challenge. The greater the promotion, the greater the attacks. It's an ultimatum, but the choice to fight is up to you.

You were rubbed with oil like an athlete—Christ's athlete— as though in preparation for an earthly match, and you agreed to take on your opponent.—Ambrose of Milan

I Command You to Fight will aid you in identifying your opponent, recognizing that people may appear to be the enemy, but our fight has never been with "flesh and blood," and there is no way to win a war if we don't know who or what we're actually fighting. I'm excited about our journey together.

Declare with me, "My life will be a living example of triumph in Jesus' name." Let's pray: "Heavenly Father, thank you for opening the eyes of our understanding (Eph. 1:18) and giving us wisdom and insight into your Word (James 1:5). Holy Spirit, you are our teacher who leads and guides us into all truth (John 16:13). Let the revelation of your Word strengthen us, equip us, and prepare us for our Kingdom assignment (Eph. 3:16). We declare that we are ready to fight, we're more than conquerors, and we have already won (Rom. 8:37)."

CHAPTER 2

A FIGHTING MENTALITY

(Prepared to Fight)

Life is a hard fight, a struggle, a wrestling with the principle of evil, hand to hand, foot to foot. Every inch of the way is disputed.—Florence Nightingale

A MENTALITY IS AN ATTITUDE, an approach, a frame of mind, or a point of view. Jesus did not come to just restore and redeem mankind, but His entire state of mind was "to destroy the works of the devil" (1 John 3:8). Our fight is a fight of faith, and we must approach every day with the mentality that the weapons of our warfare are not carnal (2 Cor. 10:4) and we have been equipped with spiritual armor (Eph. 6: 10-17). Paul declares, "Having done all, to stand." We must stand, realizing that we are "more than conquerors"—we are truly overcomers. In fact, Paul calls it a "good fight" (1 Tim. 1:18) because we have already won.

While we are called to walk in love and peace, having a peacetime mentality during a time of war convinces us to tolerate the deception of the enemy. While our message is the Gospel of peace, we must not confuse peace with acceptance. We have not been called to sit silent and passive, while Satan advances his agenda—to steal, kill, and destroy. God has placed a mandate on the Church to rise and exercise spiritual authority. We are in a time of war, but remember, we are not just fighting against flesh and blood, but against principalities, powers, world rulers of darkness, and spiritual wickedness in high places (Eph. 6:12).

Let us settle it in our minds that the Christian fight is a good fight—really good, truly good, and emphatically good. We see the struggle, but not the end; we see the campaign, but not the reward; we see the cross, but not the crown. We see a few humble, broken-spirited, penitent, praying people, enduring hardships and despised by the world; but we see not the hand of God over them, the face of God smiling on them, the kingdom of glory prepared for them. These things are yet to be revealed. Let us not judge by appearances. There are more good things about Christian warfare than we see.—J.C. Ryle, *Holiness* (Hertfordshire, England: Evangelical Press, 1989) 62

The opposite of faith is fear and the Bible declares that believers have not been given the spirit of fear, but of power, love, and a sound mind (2 Tim. 1:7). We should be on the offense, discerning the enemy's advances and positioning ourselves with authority to always be in a war mode. By the time Jesus sent the seventy disciples out to do ministry, they had been trained to believe that they had authority and they came back with the testimony that "demons were subject to them in Christ's name" (Luke 10:1-20). The Apostle Paul wrote in his letter to the Corinthians, that our weapons are not carnal, but mighty (forceful, potent, powerful, and strong) (2 Cor. 10:4). We are not timid, faint-hearted soldiers who retreat in the midst of a challenge. We are not fighting for victory—we are battling from a position of victory—"Behold, I give you the authority ... over all the power of the enemy, and nothing shall by any means hurt you" (Luke 10:19 NKJV).

According to the first three chapters of Ephesians, we are commanded to hold on to what has been given to us—

But God, who is rich in mercy, because of His great love with which He loved us, even when we were dead in trespasses, made us alive together with Christ (by grace you have been saved), and raised us up together, and made us sit together in the heavenly places in Christ Jesus, that in the ages to come He might show the exceeding riches of His grace in His kindness toward us in Christ Jesus. For by grace you have been saved through faith, and that not of yourselves; it is the gift of God, not of works, lest anyone should boast. For we are His workmanship, created in Christ Jesus for good works, which God prepared beforehand that we should walk in them. (Eph. 2:4-10)

We must believe (have faith, be certain, and have confidence) that God has equipped us with everything we need to maintain our victory. At all times and in every situation, our faith must be in God. Our fight is actually a fight of our faith and our ability to truly believe and stand on His Word. It is more than just declaring Isaiah 55:11, "So shall My Word be that goes forth from My mouth; It shall not return to Me void, But it shall accomplish what I please, And it shall prosper in the thing for which I sent it." God is not only backing His Word, He declares in Jeremiah 1:12 that He watches over His word to perform it.

I wish I could tell you that all you have to do is quote the Word of God; however, faith that can't be tested—can't be trusted. The Apostle James exhorts us to embrace trials and testing with joy, "Because you know that the testing of your faith develops perseverance. Perseverance must finish its work (assignment) so that you may be mature and complete, not lacking anything" (James 1:3-5 NIV 1984). To persevere means to be determined, persistent, insistent, and tenacious.

You will never mature (be developed, established, seasoned) until you stop running from every storm, wilderness, crisis, or valley and allow God to develop your spiritual muscles.

The Apostle Paul wrote a letter to the church at Philippi to encourage them to stay faithful through the transformation process of becoming like Christ—"Being confident of this very thing, that He who has begun a good work in you will complete it until the day of Jesus Christ" (Phil. 1:6 NKJV).

How do you develop a "warring mentality"? The answer can be found in Paul's letter to the church at Ephesus—

Finally, my brethren, be strong in the Lord and in the power of His might. Put on the whole armor of God, that you may be able to stand against the wiles of the devil. For we do not wrestle against flesh and blood, but against principalities, against powers, against the rulers of the darkness of this age, against spiritual hosts of wickedness in the heavenly places. Therefore take up the whole armor of God, that you may be able to withstand in the evil day, and having done all, to stand. Stand therefore, having girded your waist with truth, having put on the breastplate of righteousness, and having shod your feet with the preparation of the gospel of peace; above all, taking the shield of faith with which you will be able to quench all the fiery darts of the wicked one. And take the helmet of salvation, and the sword of the Spirit, which is the word of God. (Eph. 6:10-17)

It starts with recognizing that you're in a spiritual fight that has already been won. What is spiritual warfare? It is a battle between the Kingdom of God and the kingdom of darkness; a battle of wills between God and Satan; light overtaking darkness and truth prevailing over lies. To be strong in the Lord is to embrace the truth that Satan's defeat was accomplished on the cross. As believers, we are positioned in Christ and our sufficiency and dependency is in Christ and not in ourselves.

In the Old Testament, David, king of Israel, is a good example of what can happen when we deceive ourselves and begin to think that we, in and of ourselves, are successful, prosperous, and complete, without the empowering presence of God. The people celebrated King David for his military accomplishments, so David, full of pride, decided to find out how strong he was, not comprehending that his strength was not a result of how large his troop was, but of the power of a covenant keeping God—

> *Now Satan stood up against Israel, and moved David to number Israel. So David said to Joab and to the leaders of the people, "Go, number Israel from Beersheba to Dan, and bring the number of them to me that I may know it."* (1 Chron. 21:1-2)

God judged David and over 70,000 died as a result of his sin. Psalm 147 declares—

> *He does not delight in the strength of the horse; He takes no pleasure in the legs of a man. The Lord takes pleasure in those who fear Him, in those who hope in His mercy. (Ps. 147:10-11)*

READY FOR BATTLE

In his letter to believers in the church at Corinth, the Apostle Paul exhorted them to stand firm in the Lord—

> *Not that we are sufficient of ourselves to think of anything as being from ourselves, but our sufficiency is from God.* (2 Cor. 3:5)

Soldiers ready for battle armed themselves physically in preparation for war. Spiritual warfare requires us to be equipped and ready to fight. The "evil day" that Paul writes about are the days when everything is going well and the days when all hell breaks loose. The enemy is waiting for opportunities to deceive you, discourage you, and derail you from your purpose and destiny. The Apostle Peter wrote a warning to believers of all ages—

> *Be sober, be vigilant; because your adversary the devil walks about like a roaring lion, seeking whom he may devour. Resist him, steadfast in the faith.* (1 Pet. 5:8-9)

I have personally been on a safari in Kenya, when lions were roaming around looking for their next unsuspecting meal. Sadly, the jungle is full of prey and it was not long before a lion eyed a pack of gazelles minding their own business. I was in awe as I watched the lion strategically target a particular gazelle that could not keep up with the pack and lagged behind. The lion crouched in the grass, as if he was a house cat and at the "opportune time," he grabbed the gazelle, shook it, and the rest is history. What was my takeaway? Several came to mind: (1) there is never a time that we can become so comfortable that we let our guard down and become targets, (2) the gazelle that could not keep up was isolated and therefore became an easy victim, and (3) our enemy is always watching and observing for a time when we are unsuspecting.

With an urgency, Paul commands us to spiritually dress for battle—"Therefore take up the whole armor of God, that you may be able to withstand in the evil day, and having done all, to stand. Stand therefore, having girded your waist with truth" (Eph. 6:13-14).

> *If you are to be a soldier in this army, if you are to fight victoriously in this crusade, you have to put on the entire equipment given to you. That is a rule in any army ... And that is infinitely more true in this spiritual realm and warfare with which we are concerned ... because your understanding is inadequate. It is God alone who knows your enemy, and He knows exactly the provision that is essential to you if you are to continue standing. Every single part and portion of this armor is absolutely essential; and the first thing you have to learn is that you are not in a position to pick and choose. —*

Merrill Unger, *What Demons Can Do to Saints* (Chicago: Moody Press, 1977) 51-52.

The belt of truth is an attitude of honesty, integrity, and commitment to Christ and the Word of God. You cannot resist the devil if you are not willing to take a stand against the enemy (James 4:7).

For I rejoiced greatly when brethren came and testified of the truth that is in you, just as you walk in the truth. (3 John 3)

We are living in times where there are no absolutes and truth is considered relative. The Bible is clear concerning truth—

If we say that we have fellowship with Him, and walk in darkness, we lie and do not practice the truth. But if we walk in the light as He is in the light, we have fellowship with one another, and the blood of Jesus Christ His Son cleanses us from all sin. (1 John 1:6-7)

Satan is referred to as the deceiver. The Bible states, "Now the serpent was more cunning than any beast of the field which the Lord God had made" (Gen. 3:1). His first attack on mankind was deception in the garden where he distorted the command of God. He manipulates truth and disguises evil; therefore, the Apostle Paul warned Timothy—

For the time will come when they will not endure sound doctrine, but according to their own desires, because they have itching ears ... they will turn their ears away from the truth, and be turned aside to fables. (2 Tim. 4:3-4)

We wear the belt of truth to keep us from falling into the trap of disbelieving God's Word and His power. Doubt, anxiety, and worry are glaring red flags that we don't believe that God can meet us at our point of need. The belt of truth is crucial because it holds the other armor in place. When the belt of truth slips, the enemy will bring deception through confusion and lies.

The enemy is strategic in his points of attack. He is ardently after your heart; therefore, God has instructed us to guard, shield, and protect our heart by wearing the "breastplate of righteousness." The command "put on the breastplate of righteousness" (Eph. 6:14) is a mandate for believers to counteract Satan's ability to exploit whatever weaknesses he finds.

The Lord saw how great man's wickedness on the earth had become, and that every inclination of the thoughts of his heart was only evil all the time. The Lord was grieved that he had made man on the earth, and his heart was filled with pain. (Gen. 6:5-6 NIV 1984)

When Adam fell, the effects were profound—our minds, our wills, and our emotions were impacted by sin. Satan's goal has always been to negatively impact those vulnerable areas in our lives. The word "heart" is mentioned 830 times in the Bible. We have a heart because God has a heart—

After removing Saul, he made David their king. He testified concerning him: 'I have found David son of Jesse a man after my own heart; he will do everything I want him to do.' (Acts 13:22 NIV 1984)

The Roman breastplate protected the vital organ, the heart, and covered the midsection, from below the neck to the thighs.

Since our actions, works, and pursuits, all proceed from the heart, the Bible commands us to protect our hearts:

Keep your heart with all diligence, for out of it spring the issues of life. (Prov. 4:23 NKJV)

What we say and do are influenced by what we are harboring in our heart—

"Out of the abundance of the heart the mouth speaketh." (Matt. 12:34 KJV)

Let me share with you five reasons our hearts need guarding. First, our hearts need guarding because we do not think and view situations like God does.

When they arrived, Samuel saw Eliab and thought, "Surely the Lord's anointed stands here before the Lord." But the

Lord said to Samuel, "Do not consider his appearance or his height, for I have rejected him. The Lord does not look at the things man looks at. Man looks at the outward appearance, but the Lord looks at the heart." (1 Sam. 16:6-7 NIV 1984)

Secondly, our hearts need guarding because, like sheep, we want to live independently, so we wander away from the Shepherd and we take charge of our own destinies. We will trust God to take us to heaven, but we want to control our lives on earth. Thirdly, our hearts need guarding because the heart is deceitful, selfish, self-centered, and cannot be trusted.

Trust in the Lord with all your heart, and lean not on your own understanding; In all your ways acknowledge Him, And He shall direct your paths. (Prov. 3:5-6 NKJV)

Fourthly, our hearts need guarding because our motives are not always pure.

Search me, O God, and know my heart; test me and know my anxious thoughts. See if there is any offensive way in me, and lead me in the way everlasting. (Ps. 139:23-24 NIV 1984)

Finally, our hearts need to be guarded because our attitudes, values, and beliefs are birthed from it—"For as he thinks in his heart, so is he" (Prov. 23:7). Our righteousness is based upon our individual ability to confess with our mouth and believe in our heart that Jesus Christ gave his life for our sins. We exchange our sinful nature for His righteousness and we submit our lives to the lordship of Christ.

The word is near you, in your mouth and in your heart (that is, the word of faith which we preach): that if you confess with your mouth the Lord Jesus and believe in your heart that God has raised Him from the dead, you will be saved. For with the heart one believes unto righteousness, and with the mouth confession is made unto salvation. (Rom. 10:8-11)

The English word "heart" is often translated as "mind" in the Greek. We must be willing to let God change our hearts. The deceitful heart will try to make you think that (a) just because you look like you have it all together, (b) you say the right things, and (c) you act in a certain way, you're okay.

The heart is deceitful above all things and beyond cure. Who can understand it? "I the Lord search the heart and examine the mind, to reward a man according to his conduct, according to what his deeds deserve." (Jer. 17:9-10 NIV 1984)

God expects us to operate in truth and righteousness, and when we don't use our weapons, the result will be attacks and defeat. The breastplate of righteousness protects your heart from becoming: (1) a hardened or rebellious heart, (2) an offended heart, (3) a broken and wounded heart, and (4) a divided heart. The breastplate of righteousness is a spiritual weapon employed in a spiritual battle against a spiritual enemy, who has already been defeated.

When Roman soldiers advanced against the enemy, they wore leather laced up sandals or boots with sharp nails protruding from them to grip the ground for stability. In the midst of hand-to-hand combat, a trained and prepared soldier wouldn't slip, slide, or fall. Secure and stable footing is what the Bible describes in Ephesians 6—"Stand therefore ... having shod your feet with the preparation of the gospel of peace" (vv. 13, 16). "Preparation" indicates that we have been trained, that we are grounded in what we believe, and we are prepared to advance the Kingdom.

The Apostle Paul instructed the believers at Ephesus to use their faith as a weapon against their opponent—"Above all, taking the shield of faith with which you will be able to quench all the fiery darts of the wicked one" (Eph. 6:16). Roman soldiers used two shields more than any others; one was lightweight and round and it was strapped onto the forearm and used in hand-to-hand battle. The other shield was large and rectangular with hooks on the sides. This shield was big enough to cover most of the exposed body area (four feet high and two and a half feet wide), and they formed a metal wall that was not easily penetrated. The soldiers moved in formation, a line of shields, a line of soldiers behind them with swords, and one with bows and fiery arrows.

As the soldiers advanced toward their enemy, the goal was to get close enough for hand-to-hand combat. Our defense is our shield of faith, our unwavering confidence in the integrity of God's Word. The enemy shoots fiery darts of lies, disappointments, and despair to cause us to doubt God's promises, and fiery missiles of condemnation to keep us believing that we are not heirs of the Father and joint heirs with the Son, Jesus. At times, spiritual warfare can be so intense, that without the impenetrable shield of faith, we could succumb to the tricks, plots, and schemes of the devil.

The psalmist declares that God is our everlasting shield—

Every word of God is pure; He is a <u>shield </u>to those who put their trust in Him. (Prov. 30:5)

But You, O Lord, are a <u>shield </u>for me, My glory and the One who lifts up my head. (Ps. 3:3)

My high tower and my deliverer, My <u>shield </u>and the One in whom I take refuge. (Ps. 144:2)

Faith is many-sided. There is generally at the beginning a good deal of admixture in what we call our faith; there is a good deal of the flesh that we are not aware of. And as we begin to learn these things, and as we go on with the process, God puts us through His testing times. He tests us by trials as if by fire in order that the things which do not belong to the essences of faith my fall off.

We may think that our faith is perfect and that we can stand up against anything. Then suddenly a trial comes and we find that we fail. Why? Well that is just an indication that the trust element in our faith needs to be developed.

The more we experience these things [trials], the more we learn to trust God. –Martyn Lloyd-Jones, *Spiritual Depression,*

I COMMAND YOU TO FIGHT

Paul commands us to "pick up" the shield of faith, which places the responsibility on us as believers. When we activate our shield of faith in obedience to the Word of God, it will extinguish the flaming arrows of the deceiver.

How does the enemy attack our faith? Satan does so, by attacking our minds. Joyce Meyer summarized the situation—

So far we have seen that: (1) we are engaged in a war, (2) our enemy is Satan, (3) the mind is the battlefield, (4) the devil works diligently to set up strongholds in our mind, (5) he does it through strategy and deceit (through well-laid plans and deliberate deception), and (6) he is in no hurry; he takes his time to work out his plan.— Battlefield of the Mind, Tulsa, OK: Harrison House, 1995, 16.

Roman soldiers wore helmets made of cast metal and leather, to protect their heads from arrows and broadswords. Broadswords were helmets with handles used by the soldiers in hand-to-hand battle to crush the heads of their opponents. The helmet protected the head physically, which if injured, would impact motor skills, influence thought processes, and truly affect the outcome of the battle.

The Apostle Paul understood the importance of protecting the mind in the midst of a spiritual battle, so he wrote, "And take the helmet of salvation" (Eph. 6:17). Why "salvation"? The word "salvation" can be defined as: redemption or deliverance from the penalty and power of sin.

Knowing that you were not redeemed with corruptible things, like silver or gold ... but with the precious blood of Christ, as of a lamb without blemish and without spot. (1 Pet. 1:18-19)

He has delivered us from the power of darkness and conveyed us into the kingdom of the Son of His love, in whom we have redemption through His blood, the forgiveness of sins. (Col. 1:13-14)

However, salvation is not a one-time occurrence; we have been saved through justification from the penalty of sin—

For by grace you have been saved through faith, and that not of yourselves; it is the gift of God. (Eph. 2:8)

I have been crucified with Christ; it is no longer I who live, but Christ lives in me; and the life which I now live in the flesh I live by faith in the Son of God, who loved me and gave Himself for me. (Gal. 2:20)

Daily we live free from the power of sin and the ongoing attacks of the devil through the process of sanctification—

For the message of the cross is foolishness to those who are perishing, but to us who are being saved it is the power of God. (1 Cor. 1:18)

For sin shall not have dominion over you, for you are not under law but under grace. (Rom. 6:14)

As believers we are preserved secure in our eternal glorification—

Who are kept by the power of God through faith for salvation ready to be revealed in the last time. (1 Pet. 1:5)

For I consider that the sufferings of this present time are not worthy to be compared with the glory which shall be revealed in us. (Rom. 8:18)

The helmet of salvation provides assurance for believers that their salvation in Christ is secure and their position in Christ is guaranteed, despite the tormenting attacks of the enemy.

Now to Him who is able to keep you from stumbling, And to present you faultless Before the presence of His glory with exceeding joy. (Jude 24)

And raised us up together, and made us sit together in the heavenly places in Christ Jesus, that in the ages to come He might show the exceeding riches of His grace in His kindness toward us in Christ Jesus. (Eph. 2:6-7)

The helmet of salvation acts to "counteract" the mental warfare that takes place when you're battling thoughts of depression, discouragement, and doubt—the big three D's. When the enemy can get you to doubt your salvation, he recognizes that you will begin to doubt the promises of God, which include God's protection, peace, and the provision. As believers, you and I must be assured that—"being confident of this very thing, that He who has begun a good work in you will complete it until the day of Jesus Christ" (Phil. 1:6). When the enemy attacks, the helmet of salvation empowers the believer to stand and endure, not faint and give in—"If you faint in the day of adversity, your strength is small" (Prov. 24:10).

Satan works overtime to gain access to your thoughts. He wants to control, influence, and torment your mind. The moment you start to renew your mind, literally, all hell breaks loose and the enemy doesn't know what to do with you. Instead of being an accident going somewhere to happen, you become a threat to the enemy—

I beseech you therefore, brethren, by the mercies of God, that you present your bodies a living sacrifice, holy, acceptable to God, which is your reasonable service. And do not be conformed to this world, but be transformed by the renewing of your mind, that you may prove what is that good and acceptable and perfect will of God. (Rom. 12:1-2)

Every time I read that Scripture, I think about the lambs, goats, and bullocks that were slain as burnt offerings. They were captured, tied down, and killed, and their blood was shed for the sins of the people. In contrast, God is not asking us to die. Jesus, the lamb without sin, did that for us. Our responsibility is to surrender our lives to establish the Kingdom of God. The Apostle Paul reminds us that we have been bought with the precious blood of Jesus, and our lives are no longer our own.

Inquiring minds want to know, "Why the renewing of our minds?" The answer is easy: "That's where the real battle is." If the devil can control your thoughts, manipulate your emotions, influence your behavior, and confuse your thinking—then he can affect your actions and neutralize your effectiveness. I have to declare that I have the mind of Christ, on a regular basis. In fact the Word of God commands us to take on the mind of Christ—"Let this mind be in you which was also in Christ Jesus" (Phil. 2:5 NKJV). Did you notice that you have a choice and God will never force His will on you?

For though we walk in the flesh, we do not war according to the flesh. For the weapons of our warfare are not carnal but mighty in God for pulling down strongholds, casting down arguments and every high thing that exalts itself against the knowledge of God, bringing every thought into captivity to the obedience of Christ, and being ready to punish all disobedience when your obedience is fulfilled. (2 Cor. 10:3-6)

Second Corinthians shows us how critical the mind is to the outcome of an attack. You have to fight to stay in the spirit when your natural inclination is to respond in the flesh. In fact, the enemy is anticipating that your first response to any attack will always be to take matters into your own hands; instead of responding from a position of power, you respond according to your circumstances. The enemy's goal is to distort God's truth with half-truths and lies. When his deception becomes your reality, the enemy believes that you are no longer a threat.

TESTIMONY: GABRIELLA BOUDREAUX
From Bondage to Victory

Have you ever started a journey only to realize you had taken the wrong road? My journey began with what I thought was the "love of my life." At that time, I thought being married was my life's purpose. But life turned into a wild roller coaster, and then my marriage went from heaven to hell.

The amusement of marriage life ended when I first found out that the love of my life had a substance abuse problem. It affected the marriage in more ways than one. First of all, it affected the finances. The financial freedom I thought I would have being married was more like being stuck on a rollercoaster ride. I was alone at the top of the roller coaster screaming as loudly as I could, but no one could hear me. Secondly, the oneness that we shared was now broken. We were no longer a team. I was left alone and I was hurt. He was no longer the driver in this marriage so I decided to get help. I suggested he go and get counseling and confronted him with a plan. We started with a rehab plan. "Let's start over," I said, being hopeful that this would end the rollercoaster ride. After several rounds of his going in and out of rehab, my hope for the future of our marriage began to fade. When I saw him in our home using drugs, I realized this was the end of our marriage.

My thoughts were consumed with anxiety and fear. I didn't have the answers. I reached out to someone I trusted for some advice. I called my mentor. "I'm not telling you to get a divorce, but you need a season of separation to have the Holy Spirit tell you what to do." It was like finally being given permission to get off the roller coaster.

My mentor was not the only person giving me advice. A good friend called me one day, crying, saying "Gay, if you have to go home to your parents, go home in order to move forward. Right now, you're in bondage." It made me take an honest look at myself and where my life was at that time.

But let's not mistake, while I knew that I couldn't stay in the marriage, I was still afraid because I was losing this race. All that I thought I knew was about to vanish. In the meantime, several other issues began to appear. Being under stress caused me to gain weight. My skin broke out in hives.

At a low point, I had to ask for my parents to help just to keep me financially stable. Still, going back home was not an option. I was embarrassed and began to isolate myself from friends. I didn't want anyone to see what was actually taking place.

As I headed into a new phase, wanting to be in a different place in my life, I relied on my faith. My faith was always anchored in the Lord. "I can't give up," I said. I knew that it was time to fight for myself. I memorized Isaiah 54:17: "No weapon formed against you shall prosper." I stood on His Word. I didn't know anything else. Others in this kind of situation might have turned away from the Lord. I drew closer. It was always important to me to be in proper alignment with the Lord. He was everything I had then and everything I have now. I knew I was made for more than this.

I was now free from the life of bondage. Consequently, the race was not over once I crossed the finish line. My divorce was not the end of my journey. The restoration journey had just begun and still continues today. I was back in the flow of the design for my life. And below are three key ways I maintain that flow.

1. *Divine connection:* My season of life was open to opportunities that may not have been available before. As I was working at a new senior care company, a coworker saw my gift of communication. She approached me about a new job that propelled me into a life of prosperity. The Lord allowed her to open a door. Looking back she was an "angel" working on my behalf.

2. *Health and healing:* With a new focus, I took responsibility. When I started unlocking the doors on the inside of my life, I started to put my health first. The journey to health wasn't easy, but with spiritual guidance from my local church and family, I was able to conquer my dreams.

3. *Restoration:* What was being worked on the inside began to show up on the outside. I began to walk in HIS authority. I could see the light at the end of the tunnel.

Through these varied experiences, God allowed me to see that I could own and operate a business. I was approached to join a partnership and decided to do it on my own, with a friend. Opening this business on a shoestring budget, we relied on faith and were covered with prayers. God allowed all the new relationships with the job that led to the opening of my new business. Proverbs 27:17 reads, "As iron sharpens iron, so one man sharpens another" (NIV 1984). Eventually, my friends, who volunteered their professional services, became full-time employees. My business life shot off from there. Ten years later, I have successfully opened and run several profitable health care businesses throughout metro Atlanta.

At this point, I was free to put myself first. I have always had the gift of encouraging people. My sphere of influence has always articulated how I would impact them with boldness and help them take authority in their own lives. Traveling this road has allowed me to go to school to complete coaching training, which has been a lifelong dream. I love to show others that there is a better way of living. To see an individual being restored and begin to walk in their dreams, that were once dormant, gives me the greatest joy.

When I began this journey, I felt I had taken the wrong road. I now realize that God had taken me on a different path. He was leading me in a different direction. Psalm 23:3 reads, "He restores my soul" (ESV). Today, I am definitely wiser and confident. I am living my life extraordinarily and intentionally every single day.

CHAPTER 3

DEFEATING FEAR
(Courage to Stand)

Why are you so fearful? How is it that you have no faith?
(Mark 4:40-41 NKJV)

S ATAN KNOWS THAT IF HE CAN CONTROL our thoughts, he can control our actions. The goal of every believer is to have his mind renewed to the extent that he has more faith in God's Word than in what he can see—"For as he thinks in his heart, so is he" (Prov. 23:7 NKJV). The Bible commands us over three hundred times not to fear. The word "afraid" is written over two hundred times. The phrase "fear not" is used over eighty times and other word pairings: "do not be afraid," "do not fear," "be not afraid" are used over thirty times. The opposite of faith is not unbelief; the opposite of faith is fear. As mature Christians we should not need to hear God say something over three hundred times—one time should be enough.

For God has not given us a spirit of fear, but of power and of love and of a sound mind. (2 Tim. 1:7 NKJV)

Timothy had a problem. He was timid, fearful, and apprehensive. The Apostle Paul knew that if that spirit was not identified and dealt with, it would control Timothy and oppress him, and he would never accomplish all that God had called him to achieve. Paul reminded him (and I want to remind you who are reading this book), that the presence of the Holy Spirit brings power (Acts 1:8; Eph. 3:20-21; Phil. 4:13). Paul uses this word "power" in all but one of his letters. God's presence will empower you to do the miraculous. As believers we are commanded to demonstrate love and walk in the love of God that never fails (1 John 4:7-8, 10-12; 1 Cor. 13:1-8). The Word of God declares that we have the mind of Christ, so a "sound mind" is a disciplined mind that operates in self-control (Phil. 2:5; Gal. 5:22).

I Command You to Fight is for believers who have allowed fear to paralyze them. Where would you be today, had you not allowed fear to overtake you? What would you have accomplished? How many opportunities did you let pass you by? How many dreams did you abort? The Bible is full of examples of individuals who operated under the spirit of fear. Jesus challenged the faith of disciples every time they operated in fear.

FAITH BUILDING STORM

On the same day, when evening had come, He said to them, "Let us cross over to the other side." Now when they had left the multitude, they took Him along in the boat as He was. And other little boats were also with Him. And a great windstorm arose, and the waves beat into the boat, so that it was already filling. But He was in the stern, asleep on a pillow. And they awoke Him and said to Him, "Teacher, do You not care that we are perishing?" Then He arose and rebuked the wind, and said to the sea, "Peace, be still!" And the wind ceased and there was a great calm. But He said to them, "Why are you so fearful? How is it that you have no faith?" And they feared exceedingly, and said to one another, "Who can this be, that even the wind and the sea obey Him!"
(Mark 4:35-41 NKJV)

This is a very familiar story to many of us; however, I want us to focus on some key facts that can radically change how you view and gain victory over your storms. First, Jesus and the disciples were completing an aggressive expedition and everyone was exhausted, to the point of passing out. It was night and in a matter of moments the Sea of Galilee went from being calm to furious and experienced fishermen went from being fearless to fainthearted—fatigued, confused, visionless, and desperate.

Secondly, the disciples' faith had never been truly tested. Yes, they all stepped out on faith and quit their day jobs; yes, they had chosen to follow a man based upon the "truths" He spoke; and yes, they had been obedient. He said, "Let's go," and they got into the boat, without debating, praying, or hesitation.

I Command You to Fight is about facing your fears, standing your ground, and buckling your seatbelt, because you are in for the ride of your life, but if you have heard the voice of God, I want you to hold on to these words—"Let us cross over to the other side." He promised to take you from where you are to your next assignment, your next promotion, or your next opportunity. Whatever happens in between, stay focused, move with intentionality, and remember, you are never alone. Repeat these words: I am not alone, Jesus is interceding for me, and the Holy Spirit is guiding me.

Thirdly, the disciples had not walked with Jesus long enough to trust in His presence and His power (and there is a difference). His presence assures me that He will be with me in the midst of whatever I'm facing, dealing with, or going through, and I am not alone. His power reassures me that He can handle whatever I'm facing, dealing with, or going through and I have already gotten the victory (even when it doesn't look like it). Let me unpack that further. You can believe that you serve a powerful God, who is able to do anything but fail, but, when "all hell breaks loose" in your life, does your faith "set your mind at rest" to the point that you can "walk through the shadow of death" and know that He is with you and you will not be defeated (Psalm 23:4)?

Fourthly, it was obvious that the disciples had not yet come to the conclusion that Jesus was God who had come to dwell in the form of flesh (John 1:14). In their distress, they yelled for Him to wake up and do something before they all "perished." The fact that He could continue to sleep in the midst of their turmoil blew their mind, and all twelve of them, stressed out and on the verge of throwing in the towel, posed the question, "Teacher, do You not care that we are perishing?" Jesus never answered them. The passage tells us that He rebuked the wind, and the wind, like a disobedient child, complied and became calm.

The Old Testament declares His power and authority—

He calms the storm, So that its waves are still. Then they are glad because they are quiet; So He guides them to their desired haven. (Ps. 107:29-30 NKJV)

You rule the raging of the sea; when its waves rise, You still them. (Ps. 89:9 NKJV)

The Lord on high is mightier than the noise of many waters, than the mighty waves of the sea. (Ps. 93:4 NKJV)

The fifth observation is the disciples' lack of trust in Jesus and to be honest, in the midst of our storm, our lack of trust in God. Life's storms help us to truly gauge our faith level—

But He said to them, "Why are you so fearful? How is it that you have no faith?" And they feared exceedingly, and said to one another, "Who can this be, that even the wind and the sea obey Him!" (Mark 14:40-41 NKJV)

When studying other translations, you find the disciples were terrified, when they realized that the "Man" in their midst had power and authority over nature. They began to question each other about the "Man," never connecting Him to the God in their midst. It was those types of events that brought Peter to later confess, "You are the Christ, the Son of the living God" (Matt. 16:16 NKJV).

STORM LESSONS

- You can be in the center of God's will and in the storm of your life at the same time.

- Faith is not an insurance package that guarantees that you will not face obstacles and opposition.

- He calls us to pick up our cross and follow Him, not search for our comfort zone.

- Until you come through a storm, a crisis, a wilderness, you will never fully know that He is able to keep you, protect you, and deliver you.

- Spiritual maturity is the process of not just surviving your storms—but allowing your storms to build your faith in and dependency on Him.

- Never let your storm affect your faith to believe what God has promised you.

HOW TO MEASURE YOUR FAITH

Our degree of fear is an indication of our degree of faith. It is interesting that four levels of faith are spoken of in the Bible—

"If then God so clothes the grass, which today is in the field and tomorrow is thrown into the oven, how much more will He clothe you, O you of little faith?" (Luke 12:28 NKJV)

When Jesus heard it, He marveled, and said to those who followed, "Assuredly, I say to you, I have not found such great faith, not even in Israel!" (Matt. 8:10 NKJV)

And he said unto them, Why are ye so fearful? how is it that ye have no faith? (Mark 4:40 KJV)

And Stephen, full of faith and power, did great wonders and signs among the people. (Acts 6:8 NKJV)

Satan doesn't want you walking, talking, or living by faith. The Apostle Paul made a powerful statement in his letter to the believers in Rome—"The just shall live by faith" (Rom. 1:17 NKJV). We are in a faith fight, and the goal of the enemy is to keep you from knowing who you are and the authority and power that has been given to you through your covenant relationship with Christ Jesus.

PRINCIPLES OF FEAR

King Saul's behavior under pressure provides us with five principles of fear.

Fear Defeats God's People

Then the Philistines gathered together to fight with Israel, thirty thousand chariots and six thousand horsemen, and people as the sand which is on the seashore in multitude. And they came up and encamped in Michmash, to the east of Beth Aven. When the men of Israel <u>saw that they were in danger</u> (for the people were distressed), then the people hid in caves, in thickets, in rocks, in holes, and in pits. (1 Sam. 13:5-6 NKJV)

Fear is contagious, spreads quickly, erodes our faith, and influences our decisions. When fear turns into panic, it overpowers, overwhelms, and overcomes a person, and despair sets in.

Fear Violates God's Principles

As for Saul, he was still in Gilgal, and all the people followed him trembling. Then he waited seven days, according to the time set by Samuel. But Samuel did not come to Gilgal; and the people were scattered from him. So Saul said, "Bring a burnt offering and peace offerings here to me." And he offered the burnt offering. Now it happened, as soon as he had finished presenting the burnt offering, that Samuel came; and Saul went out to meet him, that he might greet him. And Samuel said, "What have you done?" Saul said,

"When I saw that the people were scattered from me, and that you did not come within the days appointed, and that the Philistines gathered together at Michmash, then I said, 'The Philistines will now come down on me at Gilgal, and I have not made supplication to the Lord.' <u>Therefore I felt compelled</u>, and offered a burnt offering." (1 Sam. 13:7-12 NKJV)

Samuel did keep his word and returned before the end of the seventh day, but Saul became impatient when he didn't return earlier in the day and acted as a prophet, priest, and king. Saul was determined to enter into battle with the Philistines without Samuel's input or directions. The role of the prophet was to pray and advise the king, but Saul didn't even attempt to send a messenger to alert the prophet.

Fear Questions God's Promises

And Samuel said to Saul, "You have done foolishly. You have not kept the commandment of the Lord your God, which He commanded you. For now the Lord would have established your kingdom over Israel forever. But now your kingdom shall not continue. The Lord has sought for Himself a man after His own heart, and the Lord has commanded him to be commander over His people, because you have not kept what the Lord commanded you." (1 Sam. 13:13-14 NKJV)

As the Philistine forces were gathering to attack, Saul and his army could see that they were greatly outnumbered and fear quickly overshadowed the men. Samuel had promised to return within seven days, but the longer it took, the more anxious Saul became (1 Sam. 15:5-6). As his army began to dwindle, the men who remained were paralyzed with fear. At one point he had over 300,000 men under his command; now he had less than 1000 (v. 15).

If we were to be honest, most of us have panicked at some point in our lives and took matters into or own hands without seeking guidance from God. Proverbs 3:15 commands us to trust in the Lord with all our heart and not to be guided by our own wisdom or the circumstances. In fact He promises to give us direction. Unfortunately, King Saul was so terrified, he did just the opposite and decided to perform the duties of a priest, which was a grievous sin.

It is interesting how we rationalize our actions and look to blame others for our mistakes. When Samuel did return, Saul tried three times to blame others for his actions: his first accusation was against Samuel for taking too long to return; he then accused the men of leaving him, which forced him to take actions; and finally, he stated he had no other choice but to make the sacrifice.

Was God trying to test Saul's faith and patience? Hebrews 6:12 declares, "Imitate those who through faith and patience inherit the promises." The enemy called fear must be defeated in order for us to truly trust God and wait on His timing.

Fear Alters God's Purpose

And Saul said to Samuel, "But I have obeyed the voice of the Lord, and gone on the mission on which the Lord sent me, and brought back Agag king of Amalek; I have utterly destroyed the Amalekites. But the people took of the plunder, sheep and oxen, the best of the things which should have been utterly destroyed, to sacrifice to the Lord your God in Gilgal." (1 Sam. 15:20-21 NKJV)

For the second time Saul had willfully disobeyed the Lord's will. His assignment was to destroy a nation that for centuries had been wicked, but he ended up doing evil himself. When Samuel confronted him, Saul began to argue with God's servant and deny that he had done wrong. This was the second time he lied when he said, "I have obeyed" (15:13, 20); for the second time he blamed his army (vv. 15, 21); and for the second time he used a shabby excuse of dedicating the spared animals as sacrifices for the Lord (vv. 15, 21).

Fear Overshadows God's Plan

So Samuel said: "Has the Lord as great delight in burnt offerings and sacrifices, as in obeying the voice of the Lord? Behold, to obey is better than sacrifice, and to heed than the fat of rams. For rebellion is as the sin of witchcraft, and stubbornness is as iniquity and idolatry. Because you have rejected the word of the Lord, He also has rejected you from being king." (1 Sam. 15:22-23 NKJV)

The prophet ignored and rejected Saul's lies and declared that the Lord was looking for living obedience from the heart, not dead animals on the altar. His finale justification was he spared Agag and the animals because he feared the people instead of fearing the Lord and His commandment.

FEAR ACCORDING TO PAUL

The Apostle Paul wrote extensively about the challenges he faced declaring the Gospel—

I am more: in labors more abundant, in stripes above measure, in prisons more frequently, in deaths often. From the Jews five times I received forty stripes minus one. Three times I was beaten with rods; once I was stoned; three times I was shipwrecked; a night and a day I have been in the deep; in journeys often, in perils of waters, in perils of robbers, in perils of my own countrymen, in perils of the Gentiles, in perils in the city, in perils in the wilderness, in perils in the sea, in perils among false brethren; in weariness and toil, in sleeplessness often, in hunger and thirst, in fastings often, in cold and nakedness, besides the other things, what comes upon me daily: my deep concern for all the churches. (2 Cor. 11:23-29 NKJV)

The potential for fear surrounded Paul as a prisoner, on his journey to Rome to defend himself before Caesar. His appointment was God ordained, but so was the storm that threatened to end his life and all those in the ship with him. Four anchors of faith sustained Paul when everyone around him was paralyzed with fear.

ANCHOR 1. *Your Relationship With God*

But after long abstinence from food, then Paul stood in the midst of them and said, "Men, you should have listened to me, and not have sailed from Crete and incurred this disaster and loss. And now I urge you to take heart, for there will be no loss of life among you, but only of the ship. For there stood by me this night an angel of the God to whom I belong and whom I serve, saying, 'Do not be afraid, Paul; you must be brought before Caesar; and indeed God has granted you all those who sail with you.' Therefore take heart, men, for I believe God that it will be just as it was told me. However, we must run aground on a certain island." (Acts 27:21-26 NKJV)

In a storm God still speaks. He's omnipotent (all-powerful), omniscient (all-knowing), and omnipresent (everywhere at the same time). God is the master of every storm. There will never be a situation in life that He can't calm and provide perfect peace. God kept Paul in the storm, but He gave him peace.

The Lord is my light and my salvation; whom shall I fear? The Lord is the strength of my life; of whom shall I be afraid ... though an army may encamp against me, my heart shall not fear; though war may rise against me, in this I will be confident. (Ps. 27:1, 3 NKJV)

ANCHOR 2. *Faith in the Word of God*

"Saying, 'Do not be afraid, Paul; you must be brought before Caesar; and indeed God has granted you all those who sail with you.' Therefore take heart, men, for I believe God that it will be just as it was told me. However, we must run aground on a certain island." (Acts 27:24-26)

Paul was declaring his faith, trust, and confidence in God despite the intensity of the storm, the anxiety of the sailors, and his present position as a condemned prisoner.

"For I know the plans I have for you," declares the Lord, "plans to prosper you and not to harm you, plans to give you hope and a future." (Jer. 29:11 NIV)

ANCHOR 3. No Time to Jump Ship

Now when the fourteenth night had come, as we were driven up and down in the Adriatic Sea, about midnight the sailors sensed that they were drawing near some land. And they took soundings and found it to be twenty fathoms; and when they had gone a little farther, they took soundings again and found it to be fifteen fathoms. Then, fearing lest we should run aground on the rocks, they dropped four anchors from the stern, and prayed for day to come. And as the sailors were seeking to escape from the ship, when they had let down the skiff into the sea, under pretense of putting out anchors from the prow, Paul said to the centurion and the soldiers, "Unless these men stay in the ship, you cannot be saved." Then the soldiers cut away the ropes of the skiff and let it fall off. (Acts 27:27-32 NKJV)

They couldn't save themselves, they couldn't determine how they were going to be saved, and their "salvation" came as a result of totally obeying Him. As we face the storms and trials of life, we have a choice to make—do we obey God or allow what we see to determine what we do?

"When you pass through the waters, I will be with you; And through the rivers, they shall not overflow you. When you walk through the fire, you shall not be burned, nor shall the flame scorch you. For I am the Lord your God." (Isa. 43:2-3 NKJV)

ANCHOR 4. Worship God in the Midst

And as day was about to dawn, Paul implored them all to take food, saying, "Today is the fourteenth day you have waited and continued without food, and eaten nothing. Therefore I urge you to take nourishment, for this is for your survival, since not a hair will fall from the head of any of you." And when he had said these things, he took bread and gave thanks to God in the presence of them all; and when he had broken it he began to eat. Then they were all encouraged, and also took food themselves. And in all we were two hundred and seventy-six persons on the ship." (Acts 27:33-37 NKJV)

Paul realized that this was the time to demonstrate his faith in God and to encourage all those who were with him. God had prepared Paul through the many oppositions he faced. In the end, God saved two hundred and seventy-six people because of Paul.

But at midnight Paul and Silas were praying and singing hymns to God, and the prisoners were listening to them. Suddenly there was a great earthquake. (Acts 16:25-26 NKJV)

I will bless the Lord at all times; His praise shall continually be in my mouth. My soul shall make its boast in the Lord; the humble shall hear of it and be glad. Oh, magnify the Lord with me, and let us exalt His name together. I sought the Lord, and He heard me, and delivered me from all my fears. (Ps 34:1-4 NKJV)

It is interesting that fear of the future ranks as the number one fear. It is a thief that robs us of our destiny, strips us of our confidence, limits us in our pursuit of our dreams, restricts us in maximizing our potential, steals our joy, and enslaves us in mental and emotional bondage. *I Command You to Fight* is about engaging in your battle of fear and not conceding in defeat to it.

TESTIMONY: JENNIFER LITTLETON
My Fight to Walk

What happened?

During the late afternoon of June 12, 1995, I decided to catch a ride home from work with a friend and co-worker, Terri. During this time, my husband and I were sharing a car so I thought I would give him a break from having to drive through rush hour traffic from the suburbs to pick me up from work. Also, Terri wanted to go by a bookstore that focused on African-American culture, so that really appealed to me because I loved to read and picking out another book for my personal library sounded right up my alley. So, we went to the bookstore, looked around about an hour or so, selected our books, and made our purchases. We headed home afterward.

I am a "fluffy" girl, meaning I am in no ways thin. Being June, it wasn't cold outside, so I also didn't have on bulky clothing, but the seatbelt still didn't fit me in her small Toyota Corolla. This was no big deal, as I was accustomed to riding without a seatbelt and I wasn't particularly bothered by it as I had done it many times before. On our way home, we proceeded down 1-20E from the West End toward Lithonia, where we both lived. We enjoyed each other's company and we were excited about our book purchases, so we were busy chattin it up in the car on the way to my house. About a mile before reaching the Gresham Road exit, there is a huge curve in the road that results in a blind spot for any driver. As we cleared the curve, I noticed a car was stopped ahead. Since I noticed the car, I assumed Terri did too. Unfortunately, it didn't register with her until it was too late. We crashed into the vehicle ahead of us at about 60-65 mph. Because I saw the car was stopped, I responded like a driver would and tried to "brake."

The whole event happened in seconds, but I can recall the entire scene like a slow-motion movie. I remember pressing my foot to the floorboard and trying to brace myself for impact. I flew helplessly toward the windshield and somehow landed back in the bucket seat. I hit my head really hard on the windshield and blood was now streaming down my face. I can remember touching my face and afterward looking at my hands. They were bloody. I attempted to rise up and adjust myself in the car as I was in shock and my body was starting to go numb. My friend, who was safely buckled in, turned to me and said, "Are you okay?" and when she noticed I wasn't, she began to scream and cry. I must have looked a mess, based on her reaction.

I can't tell how much time passed, but eventually a woman I didn't know appeared out of nowhere. She handed me a cloth and told me to press it against the wounds on my head. She said she was a nurse and she kept asking me my name and other simple questions that seemed so irrelevant to me at the time. All I wanted to do was go to sleep, but the woman wouldn't let me, because she kept asking me so many questions. I kept asking if someone could call an ambulance, and she told me more than once that it was on the way. I tried to look down at my legs, but she would distract me from looking. I knew in my heart it wasn't good, but I just felt so sleepy. I caught a glimpse of the windshield, and I could see a few wisps of hair hanging from a broken section of the glass.

Eventually, the ambulance arrived and a man started talking to me through the passenger window. He kept asking all of the same questions the other lady asked. I thought to myself, "Why can't she tell him? I have already answered these questions." I didn't realize at the time that this was a strategy to keep me from succumbing to the grogginess I was feeling, because they didn't know the extent of my injuries at the time. The EMT instructed me step by step, which seemed easy, until he told me that they were going to have to straighten out my right leg in order for them to place me on a gurney to transport me to the waiting ambulance. He told me it was going to really hurt, and he wanted to prepare me for it.

As he began to straighten out my crumpled leg, I remember screaming, but the sharp pain soon began to subside. Immediately, while on the gurney, I started to think, "Wow, I've never noticed how blue the sky is." It just seemed more wonderful to me than I could ever remember it being. I also began to feel an amazing sense of peace and incredible gratitude. I now know it was because of God's presence. As we were on the way in the ambulance, I was given some morphine to take the edge off.

Once I arrived at the hospital and was wheeled into the emergency room, there was a flurry of activity. The hospital staff cut off one of my favorite outfits, my pantyhose, my underwear, and removed my shoes. I lay there naked and exposed as they started IVs and a catheter. The nurses talked about their day and the latest episode of a TV show with each other in between listening to the doctor's instructions and telling me to turn this way or that way. As I looked up to their faces from the gurney, I kept telling them to "please help me—my leg." I was not yet able to feel the full impact of my pain, but I knew it didn't feel right, as my whole body started going numb following the accident. According to medical experts, numbness is most often caused by damage, irritation, or compression of nerves, and I had a lot of damage. In hindsight, I don't think they needed my help to figure out what to do. The doctor asked for a name and phone number. Remarkably, I was coherent enough to tell them my husband's name and number. I can't imagine what it must have felt like for him to receive a call like that.

At some point, I was told about my obvious and potential injuries. A broken right ankle with a compound fracture (i.e., an injury in which broken bone pierces the skin, causing a risk of infection), a broken fibula, a broken femur, and other possible internal injuries. I was black and blue from head to toe, and my head was bloodied from broken glass, so they figured I may not make it. The doctors weren't entirely sure about the full extent of my injuries. Eventually, I was taken into a waiting room by myself, so the doctors could call a specialist for the emergency surgery. My husband soon walked into the room and when his eyes surveyed the obvious damage to my body, he began to tear up. I grabbed his hand and told him "no." For a few moments, I guess we switched roles. My husband seldom cries, and I am usually a big crybaby. He told me that I would soon go to surgery and that he would call my extended family in Kansas.

The purpose of the first surgery was to clean out the compound fracture of my ankle to prevent infection and to prepare it for the next course of action. They cleaned out the ankle wound, but left the wound open to prevent infection in the bones. During the second night in intensive care, the hospital took X-rays of my right hip. The X-rays revealed severe injuries. My hip was smashed to pieces and looked like sand pebbles. I spent three days and nights in intensive care. I was heavily drugged and can't remember much, but I do recall that my pastor at the time, Craig Oliver, came to visit and prayed for me and my husband.

I was scheduled for a second surgery the third day in the hospital. The surgery would be performed by an experienced orthopedic specialist by the name of Dr. William Vanderyt. Dr. Vanderyt was one of the best orthopedic surgeons in Atlanta. He definitely had his work cut out for him. He had a lot of fixin to do. I was broke and broken inside. Dr. Vanderyt did the best he could to put me physically back together again. Thankfully, I did not have any other internal injuries. The doctor seemed to think that my extra body weight may have protected my internal organs from the full impact. Dr. V inserted pins, plates, and rods to keep it all together, which I still have to this very day. I was in the hospital for a total of nine days, where I initially received the beginning stages of physical therapy—how to stand, how to sit, how to sit in a car, etc. My description of a physical therapist is a physical "terrorist." The pain was excruciating. I was only thirty-three years old. I had no idea what the future held for me.

How did you handle it?

This catastrophe was definitely a life-altering event. Dr. V recommended that I go to a rehabilitation hospital (i.e., a nursing home). Given my weight at the time, around 270 pounds, and the severity of my injuries, he told my husband that I may not walk again. He also said that he had patients who died from blood clots due to the marrow entering the blood stream from the fractures. Based on my husband's account, he threatened the doctor not to tell me his initial prognosis. He also told Dr. V that he would take care of me in our home. He told the doctor, "If you tell her that she may never walk again, she will believe it. So please don't tell her." After some struggle with my husband about the need to consult with his own patient, Dr. V reluctantly agreed to let me come home to recuperate. My husband put a bed in the kitchen and cared for me from there.

While no accident or injury ever happens at a good time, the timing of this seemed especially cruel. I had just purchased my first home exactly one month earlier on May 12, 1995, and I had been on my job slightly less than a year, which made me ineligible for the new Family Medical Leave Act (FMLA). So not only was I in physical pain, but now it had implications to impact everything else in my life. My husband was the Minister of Music for a growing ministry with a demanding schedule. Now my husband not only had to deal with the demands of the ministry, but also to provide full-time care for a greatly incapacitated wife.

At first, my feelings were just to make it from one moment to the next. Now that I was "healing," I was just beginning to digest the impact of this on my life. I didn't know when or if I would be able to return to work in the foreseeable future. Then the depression and loneliness set it. I will always be grateful to those few people who didn't forget me in my time of need. Several wonderful friends from the church (Rosie McCoy and Claudette Brantley) sent me cards, gift baskets, and someone gave me a Gameboy, which helped me to pass the time once when I grew weary of TV.

I tried not to be a cranky patient, but I wasn't always nice to my husband, who took care of everything, including all the bills and my daily care. He had to bathe and feed me as well as some other unspeakable tasks no one likes to talk about. He was a wonderful caretaker. Not only did he tend to my physical needs, but he also really listened to my complaints and tried to comfort and reassure me that everything would be alright. I just needed to trust God. The Lord also "showed out" on my behalf. During the exact weeks when I was out on unpaid leave, my employer declared a "Premium Holiday," where everyone at the Federal Reserve was relieved from paying the employee premium portion of their health insurance. This was a big deal, because I would normally have been obligated to pay this to maintain my health insurance, whether I was receiving a paycheck or not. The week I returned to work in January, 1996, the health premiums resumed. You could say this was a coincidence, but I believe that it was the Lord protecting one of His children, even if it meant blessing everyone I worked with too.

What did you do to fight?

I had a decision to make. I could either remain handicapped, or I could fight through the pain to reclaim my health in all realms—physical, mental, and spiritual. The physical terrorist, Amy, came to the house twice a week. While I knew it was for my good, I dreaded those visits. I would be exhausted, even though I only would take a few steps into the living room. Dr. V advised me that I may need a bone graft from my sternum to patch my hip because my bone was not regenerating because the gap was so large. Any and everybody who offered to pray for me, I welcomed and appreciated their petition on my behalf. I also didn't care where or who it was. One day, a stranger offered to pray for me in Piccadilly Cafeteria; God honored their prayers and the bone began to grow back and fill in the open space.

But even more than the physical, I had to reclaim my mental and spiritual stability and health, even though both were fragile. I couldn't always go to church, very seldom in fact, but I had church right there in my bed of affliction every day. I read the Bible, Christian books, and I listened every day to Daryl Coley's Album, "I'll Be with You." The inspired songs on this album helped me to make it through my ordeal and to keep my sanity. I really soaked in the meaning of the words sung by this anointed psalmist. Hearing this Word through song gave me hope, courage, reassurance, and let me know that the Lord Jesus too endured through pain and suffering for me and that He would never leave me nor forsake me. I could still give God praise, no matter what circumstance I find myself in.

How was your faith challenged?

The biggest challenge I had was believing that I could ever enjoy life again. There was no going back to the way my life was before the day of my accident. I had to go through the stages of grief for the loss. No more high heels and I now walk with a limp. My self-image is different and I live with a certain vulnerability because my body is not as strong. My right leg is not straight because my hip is misaligned, despite the best attempts to put it together again. Nevertheless, I have had to accept my new normal and understand that my life is now different, but not over. I knew that at some point, God would use what I had been through for His glory. In the years since the accident, I have truly learned to relate to the folks I read about in the Bible. We certainly gain a different understanding by experiencing night seasons rather than just hearing or reading about it. I learned that God is faithful and compassionate and He would never leave me nor forsake me.

What was the outcome?

I made it through this trial. I still have the scars and even chronic physical pain, but they are just a reminder that I can go through afflictions and trouble and survive, and even thrive. God has not held out on His many blessings to me. However, it is important to understand that if you survive, this doesn't mean you will never have another trial or challenge. But I can attest that I made it through the previous trial, so I can <u>and will make it</u> through the one I am in right now.

How are you different today?

This trial experience helped to build my faith and helped me to personally experience God's character in action. Because my physical body is not as strong as it once was, I focused more on my inner spiritual walk instead of my outer physical walk. I learned that I can always talk to God about any and everything; after all, He already knows our thoughts from afar off. I learned indescribable lessons about God's care and compassion. He will come and see about His children. I also learned to patiently wait on the Lord and to understand that sometimes healing takes time. I also know that I can praise Him in advance for the good that the trial and affliction will produce in my life (Ps. 119:46, 50, 59, 62, 71, 75, 92, 99).

CHAPTER 4

THE DANGER OF GIVING UP TOO SOON
(Beyond Your Own Strength)

W E LIVE IN A MICROWAVE SOCIETY: microwave popcorn, instant grits, instant coffee, instant cash at the ATM machines, drive through everything, take a picture of your check and "bam," it's considered deposited. Drones bring packages, the internet speeds up the processes, and "eye recognition" technology is determined to get you through lengthy airport lines. We're in the "fast and furious" age—so we think that everything God promised us has to come right now. But that's not how God operates.

We want everything premixed, precooked, and available in the twinkling of an eye. If we're not happy on jobs, we quit them. If we're not happy in the first year of marriage, we're ready to throw in the towel. If we can't obtain, after two years of graduating from college, what it took our parents twenty years to acquire, we're ready to have a meltdown. If you're going to have longevity in your marriage, fulfill your calling in ministry, excel in your job, and birth your dream—you're going to have to endure some things.

Endurance is the ability to persevere and bear up under the weight of something. Too many of us are giving up too soon, because we're tired of fighting and we're tired of waiting. Paul in his letter to Timothy, challenged him to be tenacious—

You therefore must endure hardship as a good soldier of Jesus Christ. No one engaged in warfare entangles himself with the affairs of this life, that he may please him who enlisted him as a soldier. (2 Tim. 2:3-4 NKJV)

The story of how God prepared Israel to possess the Promised Land can be found from the Book of Exodus to the Book of Joshua. When God delivered the children of Israel from bondage in Egypt, they escaped as slaves, but God's strategy was to make them into warriors. The plan was simple: take them through a process to mature their faith, develop their reverential love for God, and prepare them for warfare. The Promised Land was theirs, but they would have to dispossess the enemy before they could claim it. The children of Israel had three types of mentalities: quitters, settlers, and fighters.

QUITTERS

In Numbers 13, Moses identified twelve leaders and gave them one assignment to spy out the land and bring back the evidence of a land "flowing with milk and honey"—

Then Moses sent them to spy out the land of Canaan, and said to them, "Go up this way into the South, and go up to the mountains, and see what the land is like: whether the people who dwell in it are strong or weak, few or many; whether the land they dwell in is good or bad; whether the cities they inhabit are like camps or strongholds; whether the land is rich or poor; and whether there are forests there or not. Be of good courage. And bring some of the fruit of the land." (Num. 13:17-20 NKJV)

Ten come back with a vision of defeat, because once they saw the giants, they forgot about the promises of God.

Then they told him, and said: "We went to the land where you sent us. It truly flows with milk and honey, and this is its fruit. Nevertheless the people who dwell in the land are strong; the cities are fortified and very large; moreover we saw the descendants of Anak there. The Amalekites dwell in the land of the South; the Hittites, the Jebusites, and the Amorites dwell in the mountains; and the Canaanites dwell by the sea and along the banks of the Jordan." Then Caleb quieted the people before Moses, and said, "Let us go up at once and take possession, for we are well able to overcome it." (Num. 13:27-30 NKJV)

It was Caleb who declared, "We are well able." Caleb's name means "dog." He was considered an outsider because he was not an Israelite. He was a Gentile, who was adopted into the tribe of Judah because of his faith.

So all the congregation lifted up their voices and cried, and the people wept that night. And all the children of Israel complained against Moses and Aaron, and the whole congregation said to them, "If only we had died in the land of Egypt! Or if only we had died in this wilderness! Why has the Lord brought us to this land to fall by the sword, that our wives and children should become victims? Would it not be better for us to return to Egypt?" So they said to one another, "Let us select a leader and return to Egypt." (Num. 14:1-4 NKJV)

It's dangerous to give up too soon. If you are currently in a leadership position, you are in a position of influence, which makes you dangerous. People will follow your lead, listen to your voice, and place their confidence in you. Moses sent twelve leaders, mature men who had been given responsibility over the children of Israel. They were not neophytes. They understood their mission, and they completed their assignment; however, they failed to realize that their negative report would bring destructive results and eternal consequences. How you view your circumstances will greatly impact the outcome. In the midst of them spying out the land, the Bible never indicates that the inhabitants (the giants) ever saw them, spoke to them, or tried to intimidate them. Their fear, apprehension, and insecurity was based totally on what they saw (their perspective). You will not walk into your Promised Land without a fight. The enemy is never a person, but a "spirit" that's looking for an open door into your life.

For we do not wrestle against flesh and blood, but against principalities, against powers, against the rulers of the darkness of this age, against spiritual hosts of wickedness in the heavenly places. (Eph. 6:12 NKJV)

SETTLERS

The enemy's goal is to get you to settle for less than what God has promised you. Never make permanent decisions when you are battle fatigued. There is a set time for every promise, prophecy, and dream. How to wait on God is probably one of the most difficult lessons to learn as a believer. We get a prophecy and we think it should happen the next day, and when it doesn't happen in a week, we get concerned; three months, we get really concerned; a year, and we get worried; five years, and we think God has forgot all about us, or it was just wishful thinking. Every dream, every seed, every promise must go through a process.

You see, time tests our faith; it challenges us to prove whether we believe God or not. It is critical what we do during our waiting season. There is a set time for your word, your dream, your promise to come to pass. God has established a time for that word to be manifested. "And let us not be weary in well doing: for in due season we shall reap, if we faint not" (Gal. 6:9 KJV). That word faint means to loosen, dissolve, crack, or break down. You can actually come to your set time, be in your due season for manifestation, and because you faint, crack, dissolve, loosen, break down, you can abort your promise and settle for less.

Most believers have no idea that there were two tribes of the children of Israel that never possessed the land that God had promised them on the other side of the Jordan. The tribes of Gad and Ruben and the half tribe of Manasseh could see at a distance the land that God had promised them, but they chose to settle for what they had. Now don't miss this point: God can bless you, protect you, and enlarge your territory, even though you're walking through the wilderness, struggling in the valley, or being tossed in the midst of your storm. The Bible says that the tribes of Ruben and Gad had more territory and livestock than they knew what to do with. When they looked around and saw how God had blessed them (in the wilderness), they said to themselves, "What could be any better than this?"

Now the children of Reuben and the children of Gad had a very great multitude of livestock; and when they saw the land of Jazer and the land of Gilead, that indeed the region was a place for livestock, the children of Gad and the children of Reuben came and spoke to Moses, to Eleazar the priest, and to the leaders of the congregation, saying ... "The country which the Lord defeated before the congregation of Israel, is a land for livestock, and your servants have livestock." Therefore they said, "If we have found favor in your sight, let this land be given to your servants as a possession. Do not take us over the Jordan." (Num. 32:1-5 NKJV)

In essence, they were saying, "We don't care about the Promised Land. Don't force us to have to fight." Once they pleaded their case, they were not ready for Moses' response—

And Moses said to the children of Gad and to the children of Reuben: "Shall your brethren go to war while you sit here? Now why will you discourage the heart of the children of Israel from going over into the land which the Lord has given them? Thus your fathers did when I sent them away from Kadesh Barnea to see the land." (Num. 32:6-9 NKJV)

Any time we set out to fulfill the promises of God there will always be the temptation to settle. I guess it's easier to settle for what looks good than it is to fight for what belongs to you.

Let me be clear: you will never possess what you refuse to believe and you will never possess what you are unwilling to pursue. The tribe of Gad and the tribe of Ruben had to commit to cross over the Jordan and fight with the children of Israel, until they dispossessed their enemies and possessed the land.

Then they came near to him and said ... "But we ourselves will be <u>armed, ready </u>to go before the children of Israel until we have brought them to their place ... We will not return to our homes until every one of the children of Israel has received his inheritance. For we will not inherit with them on the other side of the Jordan and beyond, because our inheritance has fallen to us on this eastern side of the Jordan." Then Moses said to them: "If you do this thing, <u>if you arm yourselves before the Lord for the war, and all your armed</u> men cross over the Jordan before the Lord until He has driven out His enemies from before Him, and the land is subdued before the Lord, then <u>afterward you may return and be blameless before the Lord and before Israel; and this land shall be your possession before the Lord."</u> (Num. 32:16-22 NKJV)

FIGHTERS

After the death of Moses, Joshua was "handpicked" by God to take the children of Israel across the Jordan River and into their Promised Land. God appointed Joshua to accomplish three things: lead the people into the land, defeat the enemy, and claim the inheritance.

No man shall be able to stand before you all the days of your life; as I was with Moses, so I will be with you. I will not leave you nor forsake you. Be strong and of good courage, for to this people you shall divide as an inheritance the land which I swore to their fathers to give them. (Josh. 1:5-6 NKJV)

Notice that God did not tell Joshua how he would accomplish this task, only the promise that He would be with him. Keep in mind that God was repeatedly confirming that the land was already theirs. We are called to walk by faith and live by promises and not on explanations. First, God promised to take them over the Jordan and into enemy territory. *I Command You to Fight* is all about trusting and obeying God. You will never own, occupy, or retain the promises of God unless you are willing to fight for what belongs to you and keep fighting to hold on to what you already possess. Too many of us are giving in and giving out to the attacks of the enemy because we're physically drained and spiritually exhausted.

> *The ultimate cause of all spiritual depression is unbelief. For if it were not for unbelief, even the devil could do nothing. It is because we listen to the devil instead of listening to God that we go down before him and fall before his attacks.*
> —Martyn Lloyd-Jones

Joshua declared, "You shall pass over! You shall possess the land! The Lord will give it to you!" But they had to fight a series of battles to possess their Promised Land.

> *Then Joshua commanded the officers of the people, saying, "Pass through the camp and command the people, saying, 'Prepare provisions for yourselves, for within three days you will cross over this Jordan, to go in to possess the land which the Lord your God is giving you to possess.'"* (Josh. 1:10-11 NKJV)

Joshua had successfully completed the first half of his divine assignment: he had conquered the enemy and was in control of the land and the cities. Now he had to fulfill the second part of that assignment and divide the land so that each tribe could claim their inheritance. The word "inheritance" is found over fifty times in the Book of Joshua.

Then the children of Judah came to Joshua in Gilgal. And Caleb the son of Jephunneh the Kenizzite said to him: "You know the word which the Lord said to Moses the man of God concerning you and me in Kadesh Barnea. <u>I was forty years</u>

old when Moses the servant of the Lord sent me from Kadesh Barnea to spy out the land, and I brought back word to him as it was in my heart. Nevertheless my brethren who went up with me made the heart of the people melt, but I wholly followed the Lord my God. So Moses swore on that day, saying, 'Surely the land where your foot has trodden shall be your inheritance and your children's forever, because you have wholly followed the Lord my God.'

And now, behold, the Lord has kept me alive, as He said, these forty-five years, ever since the Lord spoke this word to Moses while Israel wandered in the wilderness; and now, here I am this day, eighty-five years old. As yet I am as strong this day as on the day that Moses sent me; just as my strength was then, so now is my strength for war, both for going out and for coming in. Now therefore, give me this mountain of which the Lord spoke in that day; for you heard in that day how the Anakim were there, and that the cities were great and fortified. It may be that the Lord will be with me, and I shall be able to drive them out as the Lord said." (Josh. 14:6-12 NKJV)

Aren't you tired of talking about your Promised Land and never possessing it? When God makes us a promise, he gives us the strength to see it through. God honors those who don't quit. Caleb was an overcomer because he had faith in the Lord. For forty-five years he kept the word in his heart, he wandered in the wilderness with no place to call home, he walked around the same mountain knowing it was his, as he listened to the others murmur and complain.

He suffered slavery like the other spies. He had to face the Red Sea like the other spies. He struggled through the same wilderness like the other spies. He drank water, ate manna, and got tired of cooking quail, like the other spies. A forty-five-year promise kept him strong, kept him alive, kept the vision in his mind, and kept the dream in his heart. There will always be opposition, but remember what God has promised you.

Caleb declared, give me my land, give me my reward, and give me my territory.

I want to share with you five keys to possessing your Promised Land: (1) God honors those who do not quit. We have the faith to believe, the power to act, and the courage to fight the enemy. (2) Expect resistance. If the enemy can control your mind, he can control your actions. (3) Keep the vision in front of you. Never let what you see determine what you have faith to believe. (4) Remember what God has promised you. Doubt is the first step toward defeat, because it affects every choice you make. (5) Don't let emotions dictate your movement. How you see things (perspective) determines how you act.

It was the emotion of fear and desperation that caused King Joash to seek help from the dying prophet, Elisha. King Joash was not a man of faith, but the Syrian army was coming against Israel and he panicked. The Syrians were determined to destroy Israel and assimilate the people as part of their empire.

And Elisha said to him, "Take a bow and some arrows." So he took himself a bow and some arrows. Then he said to the king of Israel, "Put your hand on the bow." So he put his hand on it, and Elisha put his hands on the king's hands. And he said, "Open the east window"; and he opened it.

Then Elisha said, "Shoot"; and he shot. And he said, "The arrow of the Lord's deliverance and the arrow of deliverance from Syria; for you must strike the Syrians at Aphek till you have destroyed them." Then he said, "Take the arrows"; so he took them. And he said to the king of Israel, "Strike the ground"; so he struck three times, and stopped. And the man of God was angry with him, and said, "You should have struck five or six times; then you would have struck Syria till you had destroyed it! But now you will strike Syria only three times." (2 Kings 13:15-19 NKJV)

First, Elisha told Joash to get a bow and arrows and prepare to shoot them. Joash had to think he was crazy, but he followed the prophet's instruction and never questioned him. What would you have done? Elisha put his hands on the king's hands, to symbolize the power from God. When Elisha commanded him to shoot an arrow toward the area where the Syrians were in control, it was symbolic of his victory over the enemy.

Elisha then told the king to take the remaining arrows and strike the ground with them; however, he never told him how many times to strike. Joash struck the ground three times, clueless that there was a method to the madness. Shooting one arrow guaranteed victory, but he had no idea that if he kept striking the ground, it would determine how many victories God would give him in the future. He struck the ground three time; half-hearted, with no passion, and no urgency. He never asked how many times or how long he should continue. He lacked spiritual insight; therefore, he limited himself to only three victories over the Syrians. This angered the Prophet Elisha, who declared to him that as a result of his lack of follow through, he had missed the opportunity to utterly destroy his enemies.

What can we learn from King Joash? What is the battle plan for us? First, when you are under attack spiritually, mentally, and physically, admit that you need help and seek guidance. Second, the who is just as important as the what. How do you determine whom you take advice from? How do you determine if the advice is correct? God is not the author of confusion and the Holy Spirit will provide us with guidance and correction. Third, there's a thin line between faith, foolishness, and presumption. There are times when what we are asked to do goes contrary to common sense and intellect. Fourth, ask God for wisdom, believe the Word, speak the Word, and never stop acting on the Word.

TESTIMONY: AISHA DANZY
"Never Give Up"

I've always sensed the presence of GOD around me: His calming spirit in calamity. His peace in turmoil. His loving kindness and undeniable joy during the most heartbreaking times. Most of all, His unfailing love that has continued to carry me.

When I was growing up, my parents did not attend church much nor did they have a strong Christian foundation, yet I had this unusual relationship with God that even my parents and siblings could not understand, but even as a child I sensed it. I was temporarily removed from my home and placed in a foster home at the age of nine, due to unstable living conditions and accusations during my parents' divorce. I held on to the peace and joy the presence of God provided me.

My parents thought I did not know what was going on, but I did. I just wasn't afraid, because there was always this presence that kept me comforted. In a stranger's home, with other foster children, I never felt alone. During family visitations, I could see my sadness in my mother's eyes, yet I kept smiling and hugging my siblings and told them everything was going to be okay.

I knew God had me there for a reason, even if they could not see it. In fact, I was intrigued by the lives of the other children, so I made friends with them. God had placed me in a home of churchgoers, and for the first time I attended church on a regular basis and even joined a children's choir.

Although I wasn't in the Jenkins' home for long, it was long enough for a few faith seeds to be planted inside my heart. Once I returned home, I knew a few gospel songs I would hear from time to time on the radio. I knew more Bible stories than most of my family, and I had a burning interest and love for Jesus the Christ. I returned home SAVED. And wanted the WHOLE world to have this newfound sense of peace, love, and joy. As I look back, I think about how God used such a terrible time for my family, a time of great sadness and broken spirits, to plant something inside me that would one day catch on fire.

I spent the next several years back home with my parents and from time to time attended church and even watched church services on television. During my teenage years I knew God, but He began to feel a little distant from me. Like most teenagers, I hung out at various nightclubs and parties and everywhere I had no business being. With a big smile and bubbly personality, I developed into a social butterfly, and life was exciting and fun. Yet, even when I knew I was in the wrong places at the wrong time, I would secretly pray for God to watch over me. I would even ask my best friend to pray with me before we hung out for the night. She was an atheist, so she found it comical that I would ask her to pray with me. I was not even sixteen and I had all the freedom any sixteen-year-old could ever ask for. Voted homecoming queen, I was popular among friends, but in my heart of hearts, I felt convicted by my actions. When no one was looking, I was having a secret affair with God.

My life changed suddenly. I was sixteen and pregnant. Here I was carrying this "sin" around for the whole world to see and to judge me. I felt more alone then I had in foster care. I kept watching the disappointing eyes of teachers, the snickering faces of my peers, and even at times feeling unwanted by my daughter's father. I went to speak to my favorite teacher, who pulled me out to a classroom trailer and told me, "If you ever tell anyone that I said what I am about to say, I am going to deny it." I chuckled a little and told her I promised not to say a thing. She proceeded to tell me, "You need to have an abortion. That baby is going to ruin your life. You are a smart girl." I walked away feeling like a dagger had just been placed in my heart. Even though the world was against me, I loved this growing baby inside of me more than anything I had ever experienced in my life. Of course I had no idea what really to expect in motherhood, but again, there was a calming spirit of joy and peace that I felt, when I was away from the world.

I went on to have my daughter three weeks prior to entering my senior year in high school. Over the last year of high school, I couldn't quite fit in. I maintained an A/B average despite the fact that certain teachers ignored me. There was always a sense of disappointment that came from every direction. From friends (and their parents), family, and teachers. I spent a lot of time alone trying to encourage myself and talking to this beautiful baby girl about all the great things life was going to bring us.

I began to wake up extra early not only to take her to a local sitter, but I figured out a small secret to success. I would attend school looking absolutely stunning. No one would be able to see what was going on inside of me, if the outside looked good. And it worked! It was almost like everyone had forgotten that I was the girl who spent eleventh grade pregnant. Even with a few rough days here and there, I was slowly establishing the new me. This secret "dress for success" landed me a job at the age of seventeen in a local insurance agency, which would later develop into a career and award me opportunities to be a successful entrepreneur.

With over twenty-two missed days in one semester, I miraculously graduated with 3.2 average and was the first to attend college in my family with the Georgia Hope Scholarship. As I registered for my college courses, I had already achieved what many thought was impossible. Although I wasn't public about the relationship I had with God, I continued to have a secret love affair. I know that it was the presence of God, who was always with me and He would continue to carry me throughout my college years. Weeks before graduating from college, I was now twenty-three years old, married to my high school sweetheart, and expecting a son. On Mother's Day, four months prior to my due date, I felt my water break and I was rushed to the hospital to give birth. I had heard about babies surviving as early as my baby boy and I figured, surely God wouldn't take the baby I could once feel growing inside of me, not on such a special day as Mother's Day. Unfortunately He did, and when I returned home, I was angry with God. For the first time, I felt that He had turned His back on me. Then for the first time in my life, I understood the Scripture about our Heavenly Father's love. The experience strengthened me to accept the most heartbreaking times throughout my life even when they have been the most difficult to understand. Fast forward, I've gone on to remain in the insurance industry for nearly twenty years. Today I am the president of largest black-owned independent agency in Atlanta. I've received an award for being one of Georgia's top producing agencies, at the time being the youngest Progressive Insurance agent within the state.

Having developed this unique sense of trust and a strong understanding of business, I now own multiple businesses from construction to now the first and only African American formal gown store in Atlanta. I feel extremely close to God in business. Every part of your business depends so much on God, that you can actually see the blessings daily. The blessings call, they walk in, they email you; it is truly the overflow of God. And behind every blessing there is a responsibility (your image, expectation, and reputation). I've learned that if I keep my eyes on God, He will help you. My latest business venture, "Fit for a Queen of Atlanta," has been by far the most rewarding. I had no experience, no formal training, no real connection to anyone in the industry, yet God continues to open doors for me. I have met Miss USA, hosted annual events, connected with some of the biggest socialites in Atlanta, and been featured on television all within our first twenty-four months. With a heart of gratitude, I am humbled to say, I would be nowhere without God.

Now at the age of thirty-seven, I look back over my life and I can start connecting the dots on how the things we experience as children shape us into the people we are now. There are times that I miss that alone feeling I had with God growing up. Whether it was in foster care or as a pregnant teen. I could feel His presence when I was removed from everyone. As we grow up, and the more successful we are, people tend to draw closer to you, making it a little difficult at times to have that same feeling of alone time. I've learned it's important to have wise advisors who can help you understand what God is doing through your life. With tons of accolades, it's hard for me to truly accept that I have done anything special or outstanding in my life. The world is simply a witness to the work of God, and I, like everyone else, remain in awe. With many more years ahead, I pray that God continues to use me and I, in return, will give Him the glory and the honor He deserves.

CHAPTER 5

ENOUGH IS ENOUGH
(Fighting Intimidation)

I *Command You to Fight* is for every believer who, as a result of "intimidation," has experienced the agony of defeat by "reacting" to the threats of the enemy. One of the definitions for intimidation is "bullying" and we are living in a time in which bullying has become a major threat in our society. I recently had a principal contact me, asking for prayer for the teens in our area. In a thirty-day period, three teens committed suicide and two of the deaths were suspected to be related to bullying. The devil is not out to inconvenience you; he is very aware of his job description and he has the skillsets to "steal, kill, and destroy" (John 10:10).

This is the story of a wicked King, Ahab (who happened to be married to Jezebel). Israel was just coming out of three years of famine when Ben-Hadad, King of Syria, decided to attack and take advantage of their troubles. The thirty-two "kings" connected with Ben-Hadad were the rulers of northern city-states. They depended on Syria for protection and prosperity. The attack against Ahab was strategically planned to bring Ahab under their control.

Now Ben-Hadad the king of Syria gathered all his forces together; thirty-two kings were with him, with horses and chariots. And he went up and besieged Samaria, and made war against it. Then he sent messengers into the city to Ahab king of Israel, and said to him, "Thus says Ben-Hadad: 'Your silver and your gold are mine; your loveliest wives and children are mine.'" And the king of Israel answered and said, "My lord, O king, just as you say, I and all that I have are yours." (1 Kings 20:1-4 NKJV)

First, Ben-Hadad demanded Ahab's wealth and family, and Ahab agreed. Can you imagine a king turning his entire family over to his enemy without a fight? Ahab was outnumbered and he succumbed to the pressure of intimidation. The enemy's strategy is to identify what is important to you and use that as a threat against you. If you are willing to cower down, he will keep you in bondage, never fighting for what rightly belongs to you. Ben-Hadad planned to hold Ahab's family hostage just to make sure Ahab didn't back out of his agreement. Ahab never sought help from the Lord, even though Elijah and other prophets were available. Second, the victory was so easy, Ben-Hadad decided to take possession of everything he had. The enemy's plan is to hijack you and place a ransom on what's important to you. Do you value your career? Are you positioned for a promotion? Are you expecting your first child? Is this the year you're claiming to be debt free?

Then the messengers came back and said, "Thus speaks Ben-Hadad, saying, 'Indeed I have sent to you, saying, "You shall deliver to me your silver and your gold, your wives and your children"; but I will send my servants to you tomorrow about this time, and they shall search your house and the houses of your servants. And it shall be, that whatever is pleasant in your eyes, they will put it in their hands and take it.'" (1 Kings 20:5-6 NKJV)

Ben-Hadad wasn't satisfied with what he had seized and wanted more. In addition to taking the king's wealth and the royal family, Ben-Hadad wanted to send officers to search all the royal buildings and take whatever they wanted! Ahab put his foot down and finally refused. Ben-Hadad was drunk when he heard that his method of intimidation against Ahab didn't work this time. The enemy is counting on you to respond like you always have, first with emotions, then indignation, and finally resignation.

Therefore he said to the messengers of Ben-Hadad, "Tell my lord the king, 'All that you sent for to your servant the first time I will do, but this thing I cannot do.'" ... And it happened when Ben-Hadad heard this message, as he and the kings were drinking at the command post, that he said to his servants, "Get ready." And they got ready to attack the city. (1 Kings 20:9, 12 NKJV)

God sent a prophet with a message of hope to Ahab, not because Ahab asked, but because He is Jehovah, the sovereign Lord of all. God promised to give Ahab victory over his enemy, despite his actions as king of Israel. This would be the second time that God would reinforce to His people that He was in control. On Mount Carmel, Jehovah demonstrated the He alone is God (1 Kings 18:36-37). Once Ahab received the message, he asked for confirmation and instructions.

Suddenly a prophet approached Ahab king of Israel, saying, "Thus says the Lord: 'Have you seen all this great multitude? Behold, I will deliver it into your hand today, and you shall know that I am the Lord.'" So Ahab said, "By whom?" And he said, "Thus says the Lord: 'By the young leaders of the provinces.'" Then he said, "Who will set the battle in order?" And he answered, "You." Then he mustered the young leaders of the provinces, and there were two hundred and thirty-two; and after them he mustered all the people, all the children of Israel—seven thousand. So they went out at noon. (1 Kings 20:13-16 NKJV)

The enemy wants you to listen to the wrong voices so that you become panic stricken— "Then he sent messengers into the city to Ahab king of Israel, and said to him, 'Thus says

Ben-Hadad ..."'"(1 Kings 20:2 NKJV). If the first messenger didn't crush him, a second messenger came—"Then the messengers came back and said, 'Thus speaks Ben-Hadad, saying ...'" (1 Kings 20:5 NKJV). The third voice was a message from God—"Thus says the Lord ..." (1 Kings 20:13) and then again in 1 Kings 20:14—"Thus says the Lord ..."

The challenge before you is, whose voice and what message will you receive? Did you notice that the prophet described what Ahab was up against? He wasn't giving a "negative confession" and he wasn't in "denial"—"Suddenly a prophet approached Ahab king of Israel, saying, 'Thus says the Lord: "Have you seen all this great multitude?"'" (1 Kings 20:13 NKJV). God was saying, "The enemy is great, but my power trumps the enemy's and before it's over, everyone will know that I am the Lord." God doesn't want us intimidated by the weapons that form against us. He wants us to know without a shadow of a doubt, that when the victory comes, no one needs to guess who did it—He did it.

Israel had been divided into a number of political districts, with leaders who were army officers. God instructed Ahab to lead the attack against Syria using the army of seven thousand men. The plan was to attack at noon, knowing that Ben-Hadad and his officers would be eating and drinking and in no condition to fight. When his scouts reported that Ahab and his soldiers were approaching the Syrian camp, Ben-Hadad was so cocky, he told the guard to take them alive. Ahab's men caught the Syrian guards by surprise and destroyed the army. Ben-Hadad jumped on his horse and escaped with his life. Ahab was victorious because he believed God's word and acted upon it.

Then these young leaders of the provinces went out of the city with the army which followed them. And each one killed his man; so the Syrians fled, and Israel pursued them; and Ben-Hadad the king of Syria escaped on a horse with the cavalry. Then the king of Israel went out and attacked the horses and chariots, and killed the Syrians with a great slaughter. And the prophet came to the king of Israel and said to him, "Go, strengthen yourself; take note, and see what you should do, for in the spring of the year the king of Syria will come up against you." (1 Kings 20:19-22 NKJV)

The prophet appeared a second time with a prophetic word of caution. The prophet reminded the king that winning the battle was not the same as winning the war. He warned him that a greater struggle was ahead of him and unless he strengthened himself by carefully planning his next move, he would be defeated. What does that mean to you and me? When we're under attack, we tend to pray more fervently, worship more passionately, and press into God. The enemy is not intimidated by our spiritual victory; in fact he is anticipating that we will go back to business as usual and let our guard down. He is waiting for an opportune time to strike again, when you least expect it and are totally unprepared for it.

And the prophet came to the king of Israel and said to him, "Go, strengthen yourself; take note, and see what you should do, for in the spring of the year the king of Syria will come up against you." (1 Kings 20:22-23 NKJV)

The Bible exposes the weaknesses of various leaders as a warning for us to never get comfortable with past victories. David was a victorious man of war, whose fame spread throughout Israel. After David had congratulated himself on the victories God had given him, Satan came against him with a new temptation that almost cost him the kingdom.

It was after Peter's declaration of who Jesus was; after he had been on the Mount of Transfiguration, as part of Jesus' inner-circle; after he had been chosen to go into the Garden of Gethsemane; after he had sworn that he would never forsake Jesus—it was after all this that Peter succumbed to pressure and denied Jesus.

Aren't you glad we serve a God who is all-knowing, all-powerful, and ever-present? According to John 16:13—"However, when He, the Spirit of truth, has come, He will guide you into all truth; for He will not speak on His own authority, but whatever He hears He will speak; and He will tell you things to come." The Holy Spirit is our Central Intelligence. God gave them an early warning in order to prepare and protect them. It is important to remember that past victories are not an indication of future conquest. The command was given to strengthen or fortify and reinforce their military force.

While Ahab was listening to God's prophet, Ben-Hadad was listening to his officers as they tried to explain why Syria was defeated. The officers of the King of Syria couldn't understand how they could have been defeated, since they had the upper hand and far outnumbered Israel. Their excuse was that the gods of the Syrians were "gods of the plains," while Israel's God was a "god of the hills." If they changed the location, it would give them the upper hand and Syria would have the victory.

Then the servants of the king of Syria said to him, "Their gods are gods of the hills. Therefore they were stronger than we; but if we fight against them in the plain, surely we will be stronger than they. So do this thing: Dismiss the kings, each from his position, and put captains in their places; and you shall muster an army like the army that you have lost, horse for horse and chariot for chariot. Then we will fight against them in the plain; surely we will be stronger than they." And he listened to their voice and did so. So it was, in the spring of the year, that Ben-Hadad mustered the Syrians and went up to Aphek to fight against Israel. And the children of Israel were mustered and given provisions, and they went against them. Now the children of Israel encamped before them like two little flocks of goats, while the Syrians filled the countryside. (1 Kings 20:23-27 NKJV)

Since the Syrians were idolaters, they were clueless concerning the God of Israel and Israel looked "like two little flocks of goats, while the Syrians filled the countryside." The only thing they could do to prepare for the attack was to fortify themselves in the God of their salvation. Their strength came as a result of their obedience and dependence on God.

> *Then a man of God came and spoke to the king of Israel, and said, "Thus says the Lord: 'Because the Syrians have said, "The Lord is God of the hills, but He is not God of the valleys," therefore I will deliver all this great multitude into your hand, and you shall know that I am the Lord.'" And they encamped opposite each other for seven days. So it was that on the seventh day the battle was joined; and the children of Israel killed one hundred thousand foot soldiers of the Syrians in one day. But the rest fled to Aphek, into the city; then a wall fell on twenty-seven thousand of the men who were left. (1 Kings 20:28-30 NKJV)*

This was the third time God had sent a prophet with a message to Ahab (20:13, 22, 28). God gave a word of assurance, that they would not be defeated in the hills, the mountains, or the valleys. The term "valley" geographically refers to "an elongated depression in the earth's surface"; however, from an emotional and spiritual perspective, the term represents a low spot in a person's life.

> *What can we learn from their experience? First, valleys are unavoidable. You may be coming out of one right now or you may be in the middle of one, or headed into one. Second, valleys are unpredictable. You can't plan them or time them. They usually come when you are unprepared. The third lesson we learn is that valleys are unbiased and no one is immune to them and they are not based upon whether you are a good or bad person. Matthew 5:45 declares "For He makes His sun rise on the evil and on the good, and sends rain on the just and on the unjust" (NKJV).*

In addition, the fourth lesson we learn is that valleys are temporary and we should be so glad that "trouble doesn't last always." There is a light at the end of your dark valley and God has called you to walk through and not be consumed in the process (Ps. 23:4). Finally, the fifth lesson we learn is that valleys have a purpose. Faith is built and tested through the valleys of life. In a valley of doubt, despair, discouragement, or defeat—our faith is tested like pure gold— "But He knows the way that I take; when He has tested me, I shall come forth as gold" (Job 23:10 NKJV).

So how do we survive our valleys and not give in to intimidation or defeat? Satan has a plot, but God has a plan. Satan is the master of hindering and intimidating God's people. He manipulates your thoughts with the lie: "You can't" and "God won't." King Ahab's enemies thought that God could only deliver them in certain locations or in certain situations. The enemy is counting on us to believe the same lie: that God is with us when we are on the mountain and everything is going well and He is able to deliver us in certain situations, but in the valley, the wilderness, or the storms of life—we are on our own. When we're unemployed, battling sickness, dealing with family crisis—He's powerless and we can't depend on Him. He is the "Great I Am"!

When we find ourselves in a valley, Psalm 23 provides us with four powerful keys to strengthen ourselves—"Yea, though I walk through the valley of the shadow of death, I will fear no evil, for You are with me, Your rod and Your staff, they comfort me" (v. 4 NKJV).

1. Refuse to be discouraged. It is the responsibility of the Shepherd to protect the sheep. God doesn't panic when we go through challenges, but based upon the psalm, neither do the sheep. Notice it says, "I walk" through the valley. It doesn't say, "I run," "I turn around," or "I fall down."

2. Refuse to operate in fear. "I will" is a matter of choice. It is a determination and a resolve to fight. God will never override your will.

3. Rely on His presence. God is with you and He promises never to leave you.

4. Rest in His comfort. When you are going through dark valleys, you don't want to talk about God, you want to talk to Him because you have a relationship.

CHAPTER 6

GOD REMEMBERS
(Waiting without Losing Hope)

I F YOU HAVE EVER FLOWN IN AN AIRPLANE and heard, "I'm sorry for the delay, but we are going to have to assume a holding pattern until further instructions," your first response is never "Praise the Lord." If you notice, flight attendants are always calm and reassuring. They have been trained to be prepared for delays. I believe that God is expecting us to be that calm when we have to endure inconveniences, short interruptions, and long delays. It is never easy to "assume a holding pattern until further notice."

The real test of faith is holding on when God is silent. All of us have faced times when it appeared as though God had forgotten us. What we do while we're waiting in a holding pattern will determine our outcome. What do you do when the answer from God is not "yes" or "no" but, "not now"? In order to survive and thrive in a holding pattern, we must understand how God views time.

Sometimes God delays the answers to our prayers so that He can get the glory.

God synchronizes His answers to accomplish His purpose. There were times during Jesus' ministry when He delayed from intervening immediately and other times when He purposely took His time. The question is not always "Do you have enough faith?" But, "Do you have enough faith to assume a holding pattern and wait for the fulfillment of the promise?"

God knows where you are and how much reserve faith you're operating on. When He calls you to complete an assignment, He equips you with everything you need to bring it to pass. It took Noah 120 years to build the ark. What most readers don't realize is that it had never, ever, ever rained. Noah didn't know what rain was and the people who were ridiculing him, mocking his family, and teasing his children, didn't know either. This is what is called in theological terms, "the law of first mentions." The law of first mentions refers to the first time a term is mentioned in the Bible. Prior to the flood, the ground received moisture from dew coming out of the ground. While Noah was building the gigantic structure, internally, he had to wonder, what am I doing, why am I doing it, and why is it taking so long? Yet the Bible says that "Noah did everything just as God commanded him" (Gen. 6:22 NIV 1984).

A) *God has not forgotten you —*

For forty days the flood kept coming on the earth, and as the waters increased they lifted the ark high above the earth ... The waters flooded the earth for a hundred and fifty days. (Gen. 7:17-18, 24 NIV 1984)

Then God <u>remembered</u> Noah, and every living thing, and all the animals that were with him in the ark. And God made a wind to pass over the earth, and the waters subsided. (Gen. 8:1 NKJV)

B) *God will honor His covenant; just assume the holding position —*

So when God destroyed the cities of the plain, he <u>remembered</u> Abraham, and he brought Lot out of the catastrophe that overthrew the cities where Lot had lived. (Gen. 19:29)

C) God will answer your prayers; just assume the holding position —

Then God <u>remembered</u> Rachel; he listened to her and opened her womb. She became pregnant and gave birth to a son and said, "God has taken away my disgrace." She named him Joseph, and said, "May the Lord add to me another son." (Gen. 30:22-24 NIV 1984)

D) God will deliver you; just assume the holding position —

God heard their groaning and he <u>remembered</u> his covenant with Abraham, with Isaac and with Jacob. So God looked on the Israelites and was concerned about them. (Exod. 2:24-25 NIV 1984)

E) God will reward your faith, just assume the holding position —

There was a certain man ... whose name was Elkanah ... He had two wives; one was called Hannah and the other Peninnah. Peninnah had children, but Hannah had none. Year after year this man went up from his town to worship ... And because the Lord had closed her womb, her rival kept provoking her in order to irritate her. This went on year after year. Whenever Hannah went up to the house of the Lord, her rival provoked her till she wept and would not eat ... Once when they had finished eating and drinking in Shiloh, Hannah stood up ... In bitterness of soul Hannah wept much and prayed to the Lord. And she made a vow, saying, "O Lord Almighty, if you will only look upon your servant's misery and remember me, and not forget your servant but give her a son, then I will give him to the Lord for all the days of his life, and no razor will ever be used on his head..." Then she went her way and ate something, and her face was no longer downcast ... and the Lord <u>remembered</u> her. So in the course of *time Hannah conceived and gave birth to a son. She named him Samuel, saying, "Because I asked the Lord for him."* (1 Sam. 1:1-20 NIV 1984)

Everyone faces problems in life, but most of us have never been taught how to deal with our issues, so we become bitter, depressed, discouraged, and disappointed. Our future becomes controlled by our circumstances. Our text deals with a woman of faith who was broken, resentful, bitter, unhappy, and defeated. Yes, she had a husband who truly loved her (that would be enough for some women). Yes, he did everything he could to make her happy, but things can't always fill the void.

You may not be able to control what happens to you, but you can control how it affects you.

Hannah was blessed, but barren. She was favored, but barren. She was loved, but barren. In biblical times, barrenness was a curse. The value of a woman increased based upon her ability to produce a male child. Not to mention, she had to share her man with another woman. I want you to picture the other wife prancing around, nine months pregnant, not once, but at least twice (the Bible says children). Keep in mind, Peninnah knew she could not compete with Hannah for Elkanah's love, so she secured her role as a baby-maker for Elkanah and a tormentor to Hannah.

I Command You to Fight is for readers who understand that timing is everything with God. I want you to think about it: Hannah could have given birth earlier to a "Tom, Dick, or Harry"—but she birthed the Prophet Samuel, who anointed the first king of Israel, Saul, and the second king, David. So I ask you, would you rather give birth to a male child or a prophet destined to change history?

If you're still pondering the question, ask Mary's cousin Elizabeth, who had accepted her fate to never give birth to a child. Again I ask, would you rather give birth to a "Jerome, Donald, or Bill" or to the son who would one day baptize Jesus, the

Savior of the world? The Bible declares that there was no one greater than John the Baptist (Matt.11:11).

Your destiny will be impacted by how you handle your emotions. Situational Depression is defined as an emotional response to: (a) disappointment, (b) loss, (c) discouragement, or (d) frustration. We will never be free to pursue our future until we are free from the pain of the present and the past.

I Command You to Fight is for every soldier who is fighting to hold on to the promises of God, for every warrior who is worshipping God with expectation, despite the length of time, and for every overcomer who believes that giving up is not an option. The story below shows the principle of not giving up.

One day a farmer's donkey fell down into a well. The animal kept crying, but the farmer couldn't get him out. Finally he decided to put the donkey out of its misery. So he invited all his neighbors to come and help fill the well with dirt. When the donkey realized what was happening, he began to scream. Then he got quiet. A few shovel loads later, the farmer looked down the well, and to his amazement—the donkey was still alive. The more dirt they threw on him, he would shake it off and step on it. They kept throwing dirt, and he kept stepping on it, until finally he stepped over the edge of the well and took off running!

I believe that Hannah was able to survive because she knew how to pray and she had the DNA of a worshipper. God has given us powerful spiritual weapons. One of the most powerful actions we can take is to pray. Spiritual warfare calls for spiritual and natural action. Our prayers must be strategic and powerful. You have to pray with the perspective that God's blessings are worth fighting for. God's Word is pregnant with power. Prayer gives us the wisdom to know how to move forward.

The Bible says that when it was time to worship, Hannah pressed her way to the house of God, ready to sacrifice. What can we learn from Hannah? It's easy to worship God when things are going well, you've got money in the bank, your teen hasn't been suspended, and your mate is the love of your life. But Hannah didn't stop going to the house to worship; she didn't stop giving to the Lord. I've seen believers give God their heart and the pastor their hand, but they went AWOL (absent without leave) when life got tough, hopes vanished, and weariness set in. It's amazing how we distance ourselves from the Source of our strength.

The devil's strategy is to convince you that you are emotionally "going through," no one understands your situation, there's nothing to praise God for, and the last thing you need is to go to church. Isolation is a tactic used by the enemy to keep you from interacting with anyone who could spiritually empower you. First Peter 5:8 warns us that the devil is like a roaring lion, looking for unsuspected victims. Remember, I shared with you my safari adventure in Kenya. Lions choose their prey by stalking fragile and weak animals that can't keep up with the pack and end up separated with no support. I watched a lion search for his victim, wait for the opportune time, and then pounce on a gazelle that lagged behind.

Let me unpack this. I was in the mall shopping and I ran into a member of our church who had not been in attendance for some time. When I asked her how she was doing and told her we missed her, she responded, "I've been going through." It is interesting that we "go through" Monday through Friday, but we go to work; on the weekend, we go through, but we get our nails done, and go out to dinner and a movie. How is it, we can build up the strength to go to the mall, but we can't press our way through to go to church?

I ask you, where can you find the corporate anointing? Where can you have an encounter with God? Where will you hear powerful praise and passionate worship? Where will you get a word of encouragement and an altar call for deliverance? The answer is, in the church! So why wouldn't the enemy want you to isolate yourself?

Satan knows that the longer you stay away from your place of worship, the easier it is to continue. The enemy is a deceiver and he assures you that you're still saved, God still loves you, and it's not about whether you go to church or not. When you tell yourself, "God understands that I'm going through," the devil answers you with, "Yes He does and He knows your heart," which means, take as much time as you need to get yourself together.

So it was, year by year, when she went up to the house of the Lord, that she provoked her; therefore she wept and did not eat. (1 Sam. 1:7 NKJV)

Worship is one of the weapons of our warfare. When you can lift up your hands with tears in your eyes and open up your mouth to praise God for His faithfulness—you will always get God's attention. Praise takes the focus off what you're dealing with, as you begin to magnify the Lord. David wrote Psalm 34 as a fugitive under tremendous pressure—

Oh, magnify the Lord with me, and let us exalt His name together. I sought the Lord, and He heard me, and delivered me from all my fears. (Ps. 34:3-4 NKJV)

You can't praise God and worry at the same time. As you magnify (enlarge) Him in your thinking, He truly becomes the "Great I Am." When you truly seek Him, as David sought the Lord, He will rescue you, provide for you, and strengthen you.

This is where the rubber meets the road. Can you bless God when your heart is breaking and you don't understand why God hasn't answered your prayers? Can you continue to pray, when it's easier to shut down and boycott going to church?

And it happened, as she continued praying before the Lord, that Eli watched her mouth. (1 Sam. 1:12 NKJV)

So let's talk about the power of prayer. Prayer is more than a supplemental weapon; it is the foundation that secures your victory. Don't miss this point: Hannah continued to pray. She didn't stop when she felt like stopping; she didn't take a break, when her circumstances didn't change; and she didn't quit bombarding heaven when God didn't respond to her request.

The Bible lets us know that we serve a God who is omniscient (all-knowing), omnipotent (all-powerful), and omnipresent (everywhere). We're not just going through spiritual aerobics; we're in relationship with the Great I Am and He hears us when we pray—

"Therefore I tell you, whatever you ask for in prayer, believe that you have received it, and it will be yours." (Mark 11:24 NIV)

This is the confidence we have in approaching God: that if we ask anything according to his will, he hears us. And if we know that he hears us—whatever we ask— we know that we have what we asked of him. (1 John 5:14-15 NIV)

"For I know the plans I have for you," declares the Lord, "plans to prosper you and not to harm you, plans to give you hope and a future. Then you will call upon me and come and pray to me, and I will listen to you." (Jer. 29:11-12 NIV)

"Call to me and I will answer you and tell you great and unsearchable things you do not know." (Jer. 33:3 NIV)

"Before they call I will answer; while they are still speaking I will hear. " (Isa. 65:24 NIV)

I Command You to Fight will empower you to "pull yourself together"—"So Hannah ate. Then she pulled herself together ... and entered the sanctuary" (1 Sam. 1:9-11 MSG).

When you know that you can get a prayer past the ceiling and into the very throne room of God and that your heavenly Father has heard you, you wait on the Lord and are encouraged (Ps. 27:14).

There are three temptations that the enemy will use to manipulate you, while you are waiting for God to move. First, you will be tempted to expect an immediate answer and be frustrated when it doesn't come. Second, you will be tempted to give up and forfeit the breakthrough that is coming. Third, you will be tempted to make it happen and leave God out of the equation.

I'm writing this for someone who is sick and tired of being sick and tired of waiting. I need you to type these Scriptures on a piece of paper and tape it on your bathroom mirror. I need you to read them daily until they get in your spirit. I need you to confess with your mouth, what you are believing in your heart.

Wait on the Lord; be of good courage, and He shall strengthen your heart; wait, I say, on the Lord! (Ps. 27:14 NKJV)

My soul, wait silently for God alone, for my expectation is from Him. He only is my rock and my salvation; He is my defense; I shall not be moved. (Ps. 62:5-6 NKJV)

Our soul waits for the Lord; He is our help and our shield. (Ps. 33:20 NKJV)

But those who wait on the Lord shall renew their strength; they shall mount up with wings like eagles, they shall run and not be weary, they shall walk and not faint. (Isa. 40:31 NKJV)

Let us hold fast the confession of our hope without wavering, for He who promised is faithful. (Heb. 10:23 NKJV)

Wait by praying because it's building up your faith. Pray expectantly because it's increasing your faith. Pray consistently because it's establishing your faith and pray scripturally because it's confirming your faith.

CHAPTER 7

IS THAT A WHITE FLAG I'M SEEING?

(Surrender Is Not an Option)

By this I know that thou favourest me, because mine enemy doth not triumph over me. (Ps. 41:11 KJV)

W E'VE ALL SEEN AN OLD WAR MOVIE in which two opposing groups were in the heat of a battle, exhausted, drained, and weary of what appeared to be a never-ending combat. At some point, the struggle to win became overwhelming and one side made a decision to wave a white flag as a sign of surrender. The white flag is a negative symbol of failure, an indication that the enemy has won. The enemy's specific goal is to get you to give up, throw in the towel, and concede defeat. If not defeat, the white flag has been used to signal a truce, an agreement to cease fire and come to an understanding.

While in the process of writing this book, I was watching an old 1990s action-packed movie, *Independence Day*, starring Will Smith. The United States was under attack from an alien nation whose methods of fighting gained them the advantage. As they forcibly advanced against our military, it appeared as if the United States might be taken over. Terrified by the sight of the alien creatures and the devastation, when the commander came face to face with the enemy, he cried out, "We can learn from each other. We can negotiate a compromise and live in peace." The humongous alien from another planet declared two words, "No peace," as it began to annihilate U.S. soldiers.

God has not called us to raise the white flag or compromise with the devil. In the midst of our warfare, we are command-ed to stand—"Therefore take up the whole armor of God that you may be able to withstand in the evil day, and having done all, to stand. Stand therefore" (Eph. 6:13-14 NKJV). We must refuse to retreat or surrender in the face of opposition. Through the empowering presence of the Holy Spirit, we have a relentless pursuit to never give up or throw in the tow-el. We're focused and moving forward, positioned for victory, not planning to retreat.

If you are in the midst of a battle today with attacks coming from every side, remember that you are not alone. The Lord of Host (Jehovah Sabaoth) is with you. In 2 Kings you will find the story of the King of Syria, who, in his frustrations, sent his army to Dothan to capture the Prophet Elisha.

Therefore he sent horses and chariots and a great army there, and they came by night and surrounded the city. And when the servant of the man of God arose early and went out, there was an army, surrounding the city with horses and chariots. And his servant said to him, "Alas, my master! What shall we do?" So he answered, "Do not fear, for those who are with us are more than those who are with them." And Elisha prayed, and said, "Lord, I pray, open his eyes that he may see." Then the Lord opened the eyes of the young man, and he saw. And behold, the mountain was full of horses and chariots of fire all around Elisha. So when the Syrians came down to him, Elisha prayed to the Lord, and

said, "Strike this people, I pray, with blindness." And He
struck them with blindness according to the word of Elisha.
(2 Kings 6:14-18 NKJV)

When Elisha's servant saw that they were surrounded with
no way to escape, he panicked. In the natural he had a right to
be concerned; they were outnumbered, they were out-skilled,
and they did not have an exit strategy. But I want you to notice that Elisha was not moved by what he saw and he never
responded with apprehension or fear. He took a spiritual approach and prayed. I know that's not what you wanted to hear.
Too often, when faced with a crisis, our M.O. (modus operan-
di) is to react, based upon:

- two of our five senses, sight and sound. The enemy is
  counting on you to make decisions based upon what
  you see.

- and the three voices that you are hearing—(a) what
  you're saying to yourself, (b) what others are saying, and
  (c) what the enemy is saying.

This is not the time to raise the white towel in defeat or throw
in the towel in frustration. When you're in the midst of a storm
and all hell is coming against you—you begin to pray without
ceasing. Remember, you're not fighting for your victory, but
you are fighting from a position of victory. What's the difference; is that just a play on words? The answer is "no." Romans 8:37 declares that we are more than conquerors through
Christ, which allows us to live in the natural and operate on a
supernatural level.

It is not enough to quote, Philippians 4:13—"I can do all
things through Christ who strengthens me." The reality is, you
can and God expects you to, because you have the empowering
presence of the Holy Spirit dwelling within you. You can walk
with your head held high, because He is the lifter of a bowed
head. You can look toward heaven and know without a shadow
of a doubt that all of your help comes from the Lord (Ps. 121).

You need to be saying "Amen" even as you read this. You can lift your head, open your mouth, and shout unto God with a voice of triumph, even if you are in the valley, the wilderness, and a storm.

When you read 1 John 4:4, it should be a reminder of your victorious position in Christ Jesus. "You are of God, little children, and have overcome them, because He who is in you is greater than he who is in the world." In one of his last intimate times with His disciples, Jesus told them that His assignment was over and He would no longer be with them, but the Comforter would take His place. The third person of the Trinity, the Holy Spirit, would reside within them to guide them, teach them, convict them, show them things to come, and empower them to overcome. He assured them (and us) that we will never have to walk alone, never have to lean unto our own understanding, and never have to fight in our own strength (John 14–16).

Where are my overcomers? Revelation 12:11 gives us one of the keys to our victory: understanding the power that's in the blood of Jesus that was shed on Calvary.

If you were to be honest, there have probably been times in your life when you have been tempted to wave the white flag. It's not that you don't love the Lord. It's not that you don't have faith. You are just tired of fighting the battles of life. You are tired of taking one step forward and two and three steps backward. You're tired of declaring and decreeing the Word of God, fighting the good fight of faith, and seeing the enemy continuing to advance. How do you continue to stand, when in the midst of fighting one battle, you come under a new attack and find yourself overwhelmed and mentally and emotionally drained?

Just having faith and trusting in the Lord seems so hard when the attacks keep coming and you are in the heat of the battle with no relief in sight. The enemy's goal is to keep you from fulfilling your destiny and accomplishing the purpose for which you were created (Jer. 1:5). Satan knows that if he can control your thoughts—he can control your actions. Your victory depends upon how you view and respond to your circumstances. From the day that the Prophet Samuel anointed David to take King Saul's place and become the second king of Israel, he found himself in one battle after another. Second Samuel 21 describes a relentless series of attacks toward the end of his reign—

Once again there was a battle between the Philistines and Israel. David went down with his men to fight against the Philistines, and he became exhausted (weak, tired, vulnerable and powerless) and Ishbi-benob, one of the descendants of Rapha, whose bronze spearhead weighed three hundred shekels and who was armed with a new sword, said he would kill David. But Abishai son of Zeruiah came to David's rescue; he struck the Philistine down and killed him. Then David's men swore to him, saying, "Never again will you go out with us to battle, so that the lamp of Israel will not be extinguished."

In the course of time, there was another battle with the Philistines, at Gob. At that time Sibbecai the Hushathite killed Saph, one of the descendants of Rapha. In another battle with the Philistines at Gob, Elhanan son of Jaare-Oregim the Bethlehemite killed Goliath the Gittite, who had a spear with a shaft like a weaver's rod. In still another battle, which took place at Gath, there was a huge man with six fingers on each hand and six toes on each foot—twenty-four in all. He also was descended from Rapha. When he taunted Israel, Jonathan son of Shimeah, David's brother, killed him. These four were descendants of Rapha in Gath, and they fell at the hands of David and his men. (2 Sam. 21:15-22)

What do you do when you find yourself struggling with a situation that you thought you had overcome? What do you do when you find yourself dealing with a challenge that you thought you'd never face again? What do you do when it seems like it is one thing after another? God's people faced real giants in the Bible. A giant is anything that stands between you and God's plan for you. A giant is anything that seems bigger than you. A giant is anything that appears stronger than you.

The Apostle John wrote to the Church that we have already overcome because of the greater one who lives within us; so beyond quoting a Scripture, we have been given the power to operate in it. The Apostle Paul commands us to be steadfast (unwavering, persistent, committed) and immovable (relentless), always abounding (prevailing and thriving) in Christ Jesus. The common denominator is "in Christ," not in our own natural strength or abilities. When your mind is under attack and the enemy is bombarding you with thoughts of fear, bitterness, and failure—neither your educational accomplishments, your ability to network, or your career experience will deliver you.

God commands us to stand firm in our faith, grounded and rooted in the Word of God (1 Cor. 16:13). Why did Paul write this letter to the Corinthians? The Corinthians' form of worship was based on emotions with a mixture of the Word of God, human philosophies, and their personal experience. As a result of their spiritual immaturity, they were not strong enough to handle spiritual warfare; therefore, their response to demonic attacks was to operate in the flesh. To be spiritually strong, you must allow the Holy Spirit to strengthen you in your inner man, renew your mind, and discipline your flesh. To the Corinthian Church, Paul declared—"Now thanks be to God who always leads us in triumph in Christ" (2 Cor. 2:14 NKJV).

Author William Hendriksen portrayed Paul's warfare—

It had been a fight against Satan; against the principalities and powers, the world-rulers of this darkness in the heavenlies; against Jewish and pagan vice and violence; against Judaism among the Galatians; against fanaticism among the Thessalonians; against contention, fornication, and litigation among the Corinthians; against incipient Gnosticism among the Ephesians and Colossians; against fightings without and fears within; and last but not least, against the law of sin and death operating within his own heart. (Exposition of Thessalonians, Timothy and Titus [Grand Rapids: Baker, 1957], p. 315)

What do you do when you read your Bible and you see what God can do and you look at your circumstances and you can't see God doing anything? The Apostle Paul gives us another perspective, because it requires us to accept the fact that no matter how much we may pray, name it and claim it, stomp on the devil, declare and decree, and cancel Satan's assignment— there are times when God's answer is "NO."

And lest I should be exalted above measure by the abundance of the revelations, a thorn in the flesh was given to me, a messenger of Satan to buffet me, lest I be exalted above measure. Concerning this thing I pleaded with the Lord three times that it might depart from me. And He said to me, "My grace is sufficient for you, for My strength is made perfect in weakness." (2 Cor. 12:7-9 NKJV)

Grace is more than God's unmerited favor. The grace of God is the empowering presence of God that empowers you to be what He's called you to be and do what He has called you to do.

It is the grace of God that enables us to do the will of God in any situation. Strengthening grace is God's power and ability to overcome. When you decide to live a totally surrendered life, that decision will be tested. God uses circumstances to teach us to trust Him and to operate in His grace.

The opposite of walking in the grace of God is walking after the flesh. A synonym for flesh is "self-sufficiency," relying on your own abilities instead of depending on God. Unfortunately, most parents begin teaching their children to be independent at an early age. We want them to grow up being able to navigate their lives. When they accept Christ as their Savior

95

and God as their Father, the rules change and as children of God, we are commanded to trust and rely on God.

We are commanded to "cast our cares upon God" (1 Pet. 5:7 NKJV). We are told that God will "supply all our needs" (Phil. 4:19). We take comfort that as a result of our relationship with God, we can ask our heavenly Father for things (John 14:13; John 15:7; John 16:23-24).

We have all learned to depend on our own strategies for getting what we want and as a result, God uses circumstances and situations to retrain us. There are times when God will say, "Yes." Yes, He'll give me the desires of my heart. Yes, He'll open doors that no man can shut. Yes, I will reap uncommon favor.

As difficult as it may be, I know the benefit of hearing "wait" and realizing that I have no other choice but to trust God's timing.

But those who wait on the Lord shall renew their strength, they shall mount up with wings like eagles, they shall run and not be weary, they shall walk and not faint. (Isa. 40:31 NKJV)

For you have need of endurance, so that after you have done the will of God, you may receive the promise. (Heb. 10:36 NKJV)

But what do you do when God says no? What is your breaking point? Do you know? Have you ever verbalized it? What would it take for you to throw in the towel?

God will allow the weight of adverse circumstances to become greater than the strength of your flesh. God will "put more on you than you can bear" when He is trying to bring you to the place of brokenness. He will allow the burden to be greater than you can bear, so that you will finally allow Him to bear it for you.

For we do not want you to be ignorant, brethren, of our trouble which came to us in Asia: that we were burdened beyond measure, above strength, so that we despaired even of life. Yes, we had the sentence of death in ourselves, that we should not trust in ourselves but in God who raises the dead. (2 Cor. 1:8-9)

God's purpose in the breaking process is to bring you to the end of your own resources, so that you will be ready to understand that He is the only resource you need in your life. God wants us to know that He doesn't just give strength—He is your Strength.

But we have this treasure in earthen vessels that the excellence of the power may be of God and not of us. We are hard-pressed on every side, yet not crushed; we are perplexed, but not in despair; persecuted, but not forsaken; struck down, but not destroyed. (2 Cor. 4:7-9 NKJV)

In the breaking process, God has no intention of helping you get stronger. He wants you to become so weak that He becomes the strength that you need in every situation.

God's way of answering His people's prayers is not by removing the pressure, but by increasing their strength to bear it. What can we learn from four words—"My grace is sufficient"?

God's grace is sufficient for you. It is all you need, and it is what you need. God's grace (His empowering presence) will take you to and through every storm, valley, and wilderness. He will carry you through the stretching times, the breaking points, the giving-up and giving-in seasons and the falling-apart days. God has promised you His grace.

No temptation has seized you except what is common to man. And God is faithful; he will not let you be tempted beyond what you can bear. But when you are tempted, he will also provide a way out so that you can stand up under it. (1 Cor. 10:13 NIV 1984)

The grace of God is your strength for permanent hardships (this is not a lack of faith). Too many of us grew up during the "Faith Movement" of the eighties. We were programmed to believe that if we had enough faith, we wouldn't go through some things. Paul's letters to the Church were for the purpose of encouraging believers to stand strong in their faith. *I Command You to Fight* is for every person whose faith is being challenged in the midst of lasting physical affliction, disabilities, or irreversible life changes. *I Command You to Fight* is for readers who are weary and wavering in their faith. This is not the time to give up. This is a comma not a period in your life. Commas are used in sentences to denote a pause, a momentary wait; but a period represents a stopping point. I declare to you that God has not forgotten you; this is just a season in time, and God does not intend for you to give in to your present situation.

CHAPTER 8

LORD, LET ME STRUGGLE
(Overcoming Failure)

Most of life's battles are fought inside ourselves, and our greatest periods of growth usually come during crises. —Robert Scheid

I T HAS BEEN SAID THAT FAITH that can't be tested can't be trusted. We preach that God is a miracle worker, but what about the miracle you needed? We preach that He's a healer, but you're still sick. We preach that He's Jehovah Jireh, your provider, but you lost your house through foreclosure. We preach that He's a deliverer, but you're still struggling with something you've not been able to get victory over.

I Command You to Fight is for every reader who understands that you don't know how strong your faith is, until you are tested beyond just quoting Scriptures. There is no testimony without a test and no victory without a battle. Faith is born out of your personal experience with God and it is measured by your ability to withstand opposition, persecution, pressure, and affliction.

The story below illustrates this very point. Jesus knew the call on Peter's life and how crucial his assignment was to the Kingdom of God. The conversation took place in an upper room, after Jesus had served the disciples their first and last communion with Him. He knew the urgency of the hour, but the disciples had no clue; therefore, they spent precious time arguing over who was the greatest among them (Luke 22:24). With no warning or apparent reason, Jesus turns to Peter and declares—

And the Lord said, "Simon, Simon! Indeed, Satan has asked for you, that he may sift you as wheat. But I have prayed for you, that your faith should not fail; and when you have returned to Me, strengthen your brethren." But he said to Him, "Lord, I am ready to go with You, both to prison and to death." Then He said, "I tell you, Peter, the rooster shall not crow this day before you will deny three times that you know Me." (Luke 22:31-34 NKJV)

Let's examine His words more closely. First, Satan didn't have the ability to attack or even touch Peter without permission. Never forget God is the Great I Am and He is in control, either allowing or ordaining everything that is taking place. He is omniscient (all-knowing), omnipotent (all-powerful), and omnipresent (everywhere). Remember that Satan's limited power forced him to get permission to touch God's elect, Job (Job 1:12–2:7), and God continues to place a hedge of protection around you. The enemy wants to attack your marriage, your family, your health, and ultimately impact your destiny.

Second, notice, Jesus never said that he (a) canceled Satan's assignment, (b) rebuked Satan, (c) blocked him, or (d) sent angels to protect Peter. Jesus made it clear, "Peter, this is a faith fight that you will not be able to avoid. In fact it's going to knock the wind out of you, but let me reassure you Peter: I prayed for you on the front end and regardless of what happens, after you get your second wind, you're going to be able to help others." That one statement alone should be enough to comfort, encourage, and inspire you to fight for what God has promised you. Jesus sits at the right hand of the Father, daily interceding for you (Rom. 8:34; Heb. 7:25)

The third observation is Jesus' response to Peter's boastful declaration of loyalty. His prophetic rebuke was not given in anger, nor was it a rejection of Peter as His disciple, but it was a forewarning to Peter, who would later lament in anguish over the fulfillment of those words. Let me assure you today that nothing in your past, present, or future has caught God by surprise, and He still has a plan and purpose for your life. As you continue to read *I Command You to Fight*, allow the Holy Spirit to empower you to get your second wind regardless of what you have gone through and rebound like a fighter hitting a punching bag.

Why was it important for Jesus to let Peter struggle? What did Jesus see in Peter that Peter could not see in himself? Peter had already shared the revelation of who Jesus was—

Simon Peter answered and said, "You are the Christ, the Son of the living God." Jesus answered and said to him, "Blessed are you, Simon Bar-Jonah, for flesh and blood has not revealed this to you, but My Father who is in heaven. And I also say to you that you are Peter, and on this rock I will build My church, and the gates of Hades shall not prevail against it. And I will give you the keys of the kingdom of heaven, and whatever you bind on earth will be bound in heaven, and whatever you loose on earth will be loosed in heaven." (Matt. 16:16-19 NKJV)

Notice that Jesus never said, "if you return to me," but "when you return." His faith was not in Peter, but in the fact that He had (past tense) already covered him in prayer. Sifting didn't destroy Peter's faith, but the sifting process strengthened him and through the breaking removed the spirit of pride.

Peter was destined to be the apostolic voice on the day of Pentecost. It was exciting to be a disciple and even more exciting to be a part of the inner circle, but under pressure, Peter struggled and in the midst of that faith fight, he chose to denounce his intimate relationship with Jesus and the disciples—

But Peter said, "Man, I do not know what you are saying!" Immediately, while he was still speaking, the rooster crowed. And the Lord turned and looked at Peter. Then Peter remembered the word of the Lord, how He had said to him, "Before the rooster crows, you will deny Me three times." So Peter went out and wept bitterly. (Luke 22:60-62 NKJV)

But Peter, after falling flat on his face, recovered from failure, embarrassment, and humiliation, got his second wind, and on the day of Pentecost the Apostle Peter "stood up"—

Then Peter stood up with the Eleven, raised his voice and addressed the crowd: "Fellow Jews and all of you who live in Jerusalem, let me explain this to you; listen carefully to what I say." (Acts 2:14 NIV)

Christ could have chosen any of the disciples to preach, but He chose Peter: Peter the liar, Peter the denier, and Peter the failure. Thousands came to Christ because of Peter's message. How did he recover? How did he stand flat-footed before the other disciples and the crowd and proclaim his total allegiance to the Gospel of Jesus Christ?

I Command You to Fight is for readers who have fallen short, screwed up, flunked out, or aborted their assignment as a result of failure. Failure is an event, not a person. If you see yourself as a failure, if your perception of your situation is that you can never recover and never rebound—you will die unfulfilled.

Pastor Andy Stanley stated, "God is using your circumstances to prepare you to accomplish his vision for your life. Your present circumstances are part of the vision. You are not wasting your time. You are not spinning your wheels. You are not wandering in the wilderness. If you are "seeking first" his kingdom—where you are—then where you are—is where he has positioned you—and he has positioned you there with a purpose in mind."

While no one volunteers to "go through," let's be honest, it has been the storms, valleys, and crisis that God has allowed us to go through that have helped us to develop a stronger relationship with God. The struggle involves what you had to fight for, what you had to fight against, and what you had to overcome. It is interesting when children take an ice skating lesson, they learn only two things in the first lesson: how to fall and how to get back up.

How important is the struggle? The story below reveals how detrimental it can be when we try to bypass the processes that help to facilitate our spiritual growth.

A little boy found a caterpillar and put it in a jar with food. One day the caterpillar climbed up the stick and started acting strangely. The boy's mother explained to him that the caterpillar was going through a metamorphosis to become a butterfly.

One day a small hole appeared in the cocoon and the butterfly started to struggle to come out. It was struggling so hard to get out. It looked like it couldn't break free. It looked desperate, and it looked like it wasn't making any progress. The boy decided to help, so he took scissors and snipped the cocoon to make the hole bigger, and the butterfly quickly emerged.

The butterfly had a swollen body and small wet wings. The boy expected the wings to dry out, enlarge, and expand so it could fly—but it didn't happen. The butterfly spent the rest of its life crawling around with a swollen body and shriveled wings.

Later the boy found out that a butterfly has to struggle—as it struggles to push its way through the tiny opening of the cocoon, fluid is pushed out of its body and into its wings. Without the struggle—the butterfly would never, ever fly.

Rick Warren, author of *What on Earth Am I Here For?* Stated, "Life is a test. God continually tests people's character, faith, obedience, integrity, and loyalty—words like, trials, temptations, refining, and testing, are used more than two hundred times."

The Prophet Jonah is an Old Testament example of failing the obedience test. What do you do when you don't want to do what God has commanded you to do? What do you do when you know what's right, but you've chosen to do what's wrong? What do you do when God's plans and your plans don't match? When God called Isaiah, he cried, "Here am I, send me." When God called Samuel, he replied, "Speak, for your servant is listening." When God called Mary, she responded, "Behold the maidservant of the Lord! Let it be to me according to your word."

But when God called Jonah, he didn't say anything. He just decided that what God said wasn't a command, that it was an option. Jonah, the prophet of God, was not in agreement with what God wanted him to do, so he willfully chose to ignore God's directive.

> *Now the word of the Lord came to Jonah the son of Amittai, saying, "Arise, go to Nineveh, that great city, and cry out against it; for their wickedness has come up before Me." But Jonah arose to flee to Tarshish from the presence of the Lord. He went down to Joppa, and found a ship going to Tarshish; so he paid the fare, and went down into it, to go with them to Tarshish from the presence of the Lord. But the Lord sent out a great wind on the sea, and there was a mighty tempest on the sea, so that the ship was about to be broken up.* (Jon. 1:1-4 NKJV)

There are four reasons why God's wrath was against Jonah. First, his attitude was wrong and he was rebellious when it came to obeying the will of God. Whether Jonah wanted to or not, God commanded the prophet to go to Israel's enemy Assyria and give the city of Nineveh the opportunity to repent. The Assyrians were cruel and wicked people who attacked Israel: killed their men, raped their women, and tortured their children. Jonah felt the destruction of Nineveh was retribution for what they had done.

Second, Jonah had the wrong attitude toward God's assignment. It was not a "take it or leave it"; disobedience was not an option.

Third, Jonah's attitude as a prophet was wrong. Jonah forgot that it was a great privilege to be a prophet and he did not have the luxury of resigning when he felt like it. Throughout biblical history other leaders contemplated giving up (Moses, Elijah, and Jeremiah), but Romans 11:29 reminds us that "God's gifts and his call are irrevocable" (NIV).

Fourth, Jonah had the wrong attitude toward God. Psalm 139:7-12 reminds us that we can never hide or run from God; however, Jonah tried and he didn't get very far. God is in control of the winds, the waves, the ship, the sailors, and even the fish in the sea.

Jonah knew that God was coming after him and there would be a consequence for his action. In fact, Jonah declared that it was God who threw him into the sea and not the sailors—

"For You cast me into the deep, into the heart of the seas, and the floods surrounded me; all Your billows and Your waves passed over me." (Jon. 2:3 NKJV)

The writer of Hebrews shares five ways to respond to discipline. According to chapter 12:5-11: (a) we can despise God's discipline and fight (v. 5); (b) we can be discouraged and faint (v. 5); (c) we can resist discipline and invite stronger discipline, possibly even death (v. 9); or (d) we can submit to God and mature in faith and love (v. 7).

I Command You to Fight is for every believer who is running from a God-given assignment or you are experiencing the consequences of being connected to someone who is out of the will of God. God will let you struggle and God will let you fail—but God will come after you. Use the six principles below to help you get back on track.

Realize why the storms are in your life.

For the men knew that he fled from the presence of the Lord, because he had told them. (Jon. 1:10 NKJV)

Realize that you play a role in your situation.

And he said to them, "Pick me up and throw me into the sea; then the sea will become calm for you. For I know that this great tempest is because of me." (Jon. 1:12 NKJV)

Don't try to keep Jonah in your life.

Nevertheless the men rowed hard to return to land, but they could not, for the sea continued to grow more tempestuous against them. (Jon. 1:13 NKJV)

Realize when you get rid of Jonah, your life will immediately get back on course.

So they picked up Jonah and threw him into the sea, and the sea ceased from its raging. (Jon. 1:15 NKJV)

God will allow us to experience unnecessary pain, if it will cause us to change.

Then Jonah prayed to the Lord his God from the fish's belly. And he said: "I cried out to the Lord because of my affliction, and He answered me." (Jon. 2:1-2 NKJV)

Fulfilling your purpose and assignment is critical to God's master plan.

Now the word of the Lord came to Jonah the second time, saying, "Arise, go to Nineveh, that great city, and preach to it the message that I tell you." So Jonah arose and went to Nineveh, according to the word of the Lord ... So the people of Nineveh believed God, proclaimed a fast, and put on sackcloth, from the greatest to the least of them ... Then God saw their works; that they turned from their evil way; and God relented from the disaster that He had said He would bring upon them, and He did not do it. (Jon. 3:1-2, 5, 10 NKJV)

What did Jonah learn from his struggles and what can we learn from Jonah's experience? First, he learned that God is in control. His will shall be done, and you can't run away from Him. Second, he learned that God is patient, compassionate, and forgiving when we repent. Third, he learned how powerful God is when he saw an entire city become repentant before the Lord. Finally, he learned how much God loves the lost and how willing He is to save them.

CHAPTER 9

STAY FOCUSED
(From Vision to Victory)

This is a war cry: "The Lord goes out to fight like a warrior; he is ready and eager for battle. He gives a war cry, a battle shout; he shows his power against his enemies." (Isa. 42:13 TEV)

THE BOOK OF NEHEMIAH provides us with a glimpse of warfare on different levels. It is the story of a man whose passion for the survival of his people placed him in a unique position to be used by God to achieve God's purposes. As a leader on a mission, Nehemiah faced major opposition trying to complete his assignment. Nehemiah shows us how to fight with one hand and stay focused and purpose-driven in the midst of coping with discouragement, false accusation, low morale, and enemy attacks.

Our story begins long before Nehemiah was born. Jewish history began with Abraham, but it was not until the people cried out for a king that Saul was chosen as the leader of the nation. Under the military leadership of King David, Israel expanded its borders and gained the respect of their neighboring allies and enemies. When David died, the throne was transferred to his young son Solomon—

Now the days of David drew near that he should die, and he charged Solomon his son, saying: "I go the way of all the earth; be strong, therefore, and prove yourself a man. And keep the charge of the Lord your God: to walk in His ways, to keep His statutes, His commandments, His judgments, and His testimonies, as it is written in the Law of Moses, that you may prosper in all that you do and wherever you turn; that the Lord may fulfill His word which He spoke concerning me, saying, 'If your sons take heed to their way, to walk before Me in truth with all their heart and with all their soul,' He said, 'you shall not lack a man on the throne of Israel.'" (1 Kings 2:1-4 NKJV)

King Solomon, who asked God for wisdom in order to correctly rule His people initially followed in the footsteps of his father, King David; however, his love for pagan women turned him away from the God of his ancestors and into worshipping foreign gods—

Therefore the Lord said to Solomon, "Because you have done this, and have not kept My covenant and My statutes, which I have commanded you, I will surely tear the kingdom away from you and give it to your servant. Nevertheless I will not do it in your days, for the sake of your father David; I will tear it out of the hand of your son. However I will not tear away the whole kingdom; I will give one tribe to your son for the sake of My servant David, and for the sake of Jerusalem which I have chosen." (1 Kings 11:11-13)

As a result of King Solomon's sins, when he died, the kingdom of Israel was split into the Northern Kingdom and the Southern Kingdom. Ten northern tribes, called Israel, migrated to the north and settled in Samaria; the other two tribes, called Judah, went south and settled in Jerusalem. When the Assyrians invaded the Northern Kingdom, Israel was taken over and the kingdom was eliminated. Judah lived in freedom as a Jewish nation until King Nebuchadnezzar of Babylon invaded Jerusalem and all Judah and took the people captive.

Jerusalem lay in ruins. The walls were destroyed around the city, the temple of God was burned down, and the treasures of Judah were seized—

And all the articles from the house of God, great and small, the treasures of the house of the Lord, and the treasures of the king and of his leaders, all these he took to Babylon. Then they burned the house of God, broke down the wall of Jerusalem, burned all its palaces with fire, and destroyed all its precious possessions. And those who escaped from the sword he carried away to Babylon, where they became servants to him and his sons until the rule of the kingdom of Persia. (2 Chronicles 36:18-20)

After the death of King Nebuchadnezzar and his wicked sons, Cyrus, king of Persia, invaded Babylon and released the Jews. It had been over one hundred years and a broken people were now free to begin the process of rebuilding their lives. Over a twenty-five year period, Jews made their way back to Jerusalem to rebuild a city and erect a temple to their God. When Nehemiah was told of the condition of the remnant who had survived captivity and had returned home to a city that had been burned with fire and without walls, he was torn with grief.

Is there anything that is taking place in our country or society today that causes your heart to ache? What emotions overtake you when you consider the moral condition of our nation, the plight of our cities, and the challenges we face in our school systems? Does righteous indignation rise up in you when you watch television, read the papers, or connect with the world on the internet and see the apathy of a nation blessed by God? Nehemiah did more than complain; he took his concern to God and bathed every move in prayer. Through prayer we regain our strength to defeat the enemy and accomplish the will of God for our generation.

And they said to me, "The survivors who are left from the captivity in the province are there in great distress and reproach. The wall of Jerusalem is also broken down, and its gates are burned with fire." So it was, when I heard these words; that I sat down and wept, and mourned for many days; I was fasting and praying before the God of heaven. (Neh. 1:3-4)

What is interesting is the fact that none of what was actually transpiring in Jerusalem impacted Nehemiah's life. He was the king's cupbearer, a prestigious position of influence and authority. He ate the food and drank whatever drink the king would drink, to ensure that it wasn't poisoned. The only one closer to the king was the queen. Nehemiah had a comfortable lifestyle, but he had a burden on his heart.

Now I had never been sad in his presence before. Therefore the king said to me, "Why is your face sad, since you are not sick? This is nothing but sorrow of heart." So I became dreadfully afraid, and said to the king, "May the king live forever! Why should my face not be sad, when the city, the place of my fathers' tombs, lies waste, and its gates are burned with fire?" Then the king said to me, "What do you request?" So I prayed to the God of heaven. And I said to the king, "If it pleases the king, and if your servant has found favor in your sight, I ask that you send me to Judah, to the city of my fathers' tombs, that I may rebuild it." (Neh. 2:1-5 NKJV)

Long before Nehemiah answered the call to lead in the rebuilding of Jerusalem's walls, God had chosen him to be a visionary leader and placed him in the right place at the right time. The king not only granted his wishes, he gave him official letters signed and sealed, and sent a military escort to ensure Nehemiah's safety. Until what grieves God grieves you, you will never have the passion or the fortitude to accomplish an assignment that requires a sacrifice and doesn't personally affect you.

I went to Jerusalem, and after staying there three days I set out during the night with a few men. I had not told anyone what my God had put in my heart to do for Jerusalem. There were no mounts with me except the one I was riding on. (Neh. 2:11-12 NIV 1984)

Whom can you trust and whom can you count on? The trip to Jerusalem took almost two months. Word began to spread that he was a man on a mission. He immediately began to survey the land and take note of the discouragement of the people. He understood the magnitude of the project and the need to rally the people. He could not expect them to see in the natural what he saw in the spirit, but as a visionary leader, he was expected to cast a vision that would compel them to unite and follow him.

The officials did not know where I had gone or what I was doing, because as yet I had said nothing to the Jews or the priests or nobles or officials or any others who would be doing the work. Then I said to them, "You see the trouble we are in: Jerusalem lies in ruins, and its gates have been burned with fire. Come, let us rebuild the wall of Jerusalem, and we will no longer be in disgrace." I also told them about the gracious hand of my God upon me and what the king had said to me. They replied, "Let us start rebuilding." So they began this good work. (Neh. 2:16-18 NIV 1984)

NO LAUGHING MATTER

But when Sanballat the Horonite, Tobiah the Ammonite official, and Geshem the Arab heard of it, they laughed at us and despised us, and said, "What is this thing that you are doing? Will you rebel against the king?" So I answered them, and said to them, "The God of heaven Himself will prosper us; therefore we His servants will arise and build, but you have no heritage or right or memorial in Jerusalem." (Neh. 2:19-20)

A "good work" will always attract the enemy. Expect resistance, but don't allow it to stop you. When you know that your footsteps are being ordered by the Lord and that God has your back, you move forward with confidence. The enemy wants you to become double-minded and begin to question your assignment. Ignore naysayers, negative thoughts, and destructive criticism.

One of the keys to Nehemiah success was his confidence in God. I caution you to be careful that you do not put your trust in your personal accomplishments—your degrees, talents, gifts, and abilities. At the end of the day, the Apostle Paul declared, "What then shall we say to these things? If God is for us, who can be against us?" (Rom. 8:31).

WHO'S ON YOUR TEAM?

Also the sons of Hassenaah built the Fish Gate; they laid its beams and hung its doors with its bolts and bars. And next to them Meremoth the son of Urijah, the son of Koz, made repairs. Next to them Meshullam the son of Berechiah, the son of Meshezabel, made repairs. Next to them Zadok the son of Baana made repairs. Next to them the Tekoites made repairs; but their nobles did not put their shoulders to the work of their Lord. (Neh. 3:3-5)

Nehemiah's one task was to strategically build the wall and to do that, he had to put the right people in position. In chapter three, Nehemiah handpicks laborers according to their skills and abilities. Notice he did not choose them based upon relationships, seniority, politics, or any of the other reasons we often choose people. Many of us are frustrated with projects and plans because we don't have the right people in the right positions with the skill sets necessary to complete the assignments. The place of agreement is the place of power.

This analogy may help you. Nehemiah was operating as a bus driver with a destination. In order to get to his end point (the completion, his purpose, goal, and objective), he had to get the right people on the bus, get the wrong people off the bus, and put the right people in the right position on the bus. Keep reading that sentence until you get the revelation. Too many times we have the wrong people in the wrong positions with the wrong skill sets or no skill sets and a bad attitude on our team and we're wondering why we are no further along.

In chapter three, Nehemiah mentions seventy-five people by name and at least fifteen different diverse groups of people. What is astonishing is that they all worked alongside one another, regardless of their titles and positions. It is interesting that he acknowledges that the nobles did not share in the work of the Lord. Don't overlook this point. We don't know why, but whatever the reason, Nehemiah didn't lament over who didn't get with the program.

What would happen if we saw our jobs (assignments) as working for the Lord? Would our productivity increase? Would our attitudes become more pleasant? What could we accomplish if we could unify under one common vision instead of multiple opinions and visions, which cause division? What would happen in your organization, your department, or your team, if those in leadership positions would create an encouraging atmosphere? Nehemiah rallied the people, cheering them on and celebrating their accomplishments.

THANK GOD FOR YOUR ENEMIES

So we built the wall, and the entire wall was joined together up to half its height, for the people had a mind to work. Now it happened, when Sanballat, Tobiah, the Arabs, the Ammonites, and the Ashdodites heard that the walls of Jerusalem were being restored and the gaps were beginning to be closed, that they became very angry, and all of them conspired together to come and attack Jerusalem and create confusion. Nevertheless we made our prayer to our God, and because of them we set a watch against them day and night. (Neh. 4:6-9)

The people had a mind (determination, confidence, and commitment) and they were not afraid to work. There is something supernatural about the power of agreement and unity; both are powerful weapons of our warfare. The enemy knows that he is no match for any group of believers who can operate in one accord. The Bible states that one can put a thousand to flight and two can put ten thousand to flight. God allowed their adversaries to challenge them and He used their opposition to strengthen Nehemiah and the people.

It is interesting how the enemy came together as a unified force to block, hinder, and impede their progress. Satan is convinced that we may talk about faith, but very few of us see obstacles as opportunities. How many of us see problems as possibilities? When was the last time you saw a setback as a set up? Nehemiah said, as a result of them, because of them, and despite them—we have a strategy.

> For the weapons of our warfare are not carnal but mighty in God for pulling down strongholds, casting down arguments and every high thing that exalts itself against the knowledge of God, bringing every thought into captivity to the obedience of Christ. (2 Cor. 10:4-5)

What was the strategy? A divine connection to their God through the weapon of prayer—corporate prayer, united prayer, and personal prayer. Nehemiah was a man of prayer, who earnestly sought God before he even began the journey —

"O Lord, I pray, please let Your ear be attentive to the prayer of Your servant, and to the prayer of Your servants who desire to fear Your name; and let Your servant prosper this day, I pray, and grant him mercy in the sight of this man." (Neh. 1:11)

Nehemiah's lifestyle of prayer was an example to those he led. He didn't talk about prayer, he prayed and after he prayed he put a plan in place. The Bible says—

> Call upon Me in the day of trouble; I will deliver you, and you shall glorify Me. (Ps. 50:15)

It shall come to pass that before they call, I will answer; and while they are still speaking, I will hear. (Isa. 65:24)

"Then you will call upon Me and go and pray to Me, and I will listen to you." (Jer. 29:12)

"Therefore I say to you, whatever things you ask when you pray, believe that you receive them, and you will have them." (Mark 11:24)

"If you abide in Me, and My words abide in you, you will ask what you desire, and it shall be done for you." (John 15:7 NKJV)

The plan was to keep it moving and not miss a beat. If your M.O. is to stop, throw in the towel, never finish, and always quit under pressure—you are right where Satan wants you to be. Intimidation is meant to slow you down, weaken your resolve, and ultimately drive you backward. Think about it. They were halfway finished. Half of the project had been completed. At the halfway point, physical weariness sets in, mental fatigue clouds your thinking, and frustration hijacks your emotions. It's an oxymoron: you're too tired to quit and too weak to throw in the towel.

Nehemiah's warfare was physical in the sense that they were fighting people (Sanballat, Tobiah, Geshem). It was also physical in the sense that they were exhausted and drained. It was also psychological and emotional—

Then Judah said, "The strength of the laborers is failing, and there is so much rubbish that we are not able to build the wall." And our adversaries said, "They will neither know nor see anything, till we come into their midst and kill them and cause the work to cease." (Neh. 4:10-11)

It's difficult to see progress when things around you don't appear to be changing. It is during those times that you must silence outside voices and internal voices. External voices can come through verbal communication or written messages, such as text messages, emails, and social media posts. Internal voices are the voices that will confirm how you really feel, despite what God's

Word declares. Your internal voice will say, "We'll never be able to do this" and ultimately you walk away with a defeated mentality. So how have you handled challenges in the past?

Nehemiah understood the mental, emotional, and physical pressure they were dealing with and yet he recognized they could not allow the warfare to be the excuse for not staying the course.

Therefore I positioned men behind the lower parts of the wall, at the openings; and I set the people according to their families, with their swords, their spears, and their bows. And I looked, and arose and said to the nobles, to the leaders, and to the rest of the people, "Do not be afraid of them. Remember the Lord, great and awesome, and fight for your brethren, your sons, your daughters, your wives, and your houses." (Neh. 4:13-14)

I Command You to Fight is not an option, not just a book, but a command. It is not based upon how you feel, what it looks like in the natural, or the circumstances you're facing. It is a choice you have to make, if you are going to fulfill your Kingdom assignment.

Nehemiah challenged the people to remember the Lord. Recall who your God is; keep in the forefront of your mind His awesome power and the reason you are fighting. You're not in warfare just to be battling, but you're fighting to complete your assignment. Your God-given assignment is what the devil is after. Now that you are saved, the enemy of your soul knows that you are only alive to fulfill a Kingdom assignment. Between birth certificate and death certificate—the dash is your life and you are held accountable for the dash. "Well done good and faithful" is an evaluation of how you stewarded the dash of your life.

And it happened, when our enemies heard that it was known to us, and that God had brought their plot to nothing, that all of us returned to the wall, everyone to his work ... Wherever you hear the sound of the trumpet, rally to us there. Our God will fight for us. (Neh. 4:14-15, 20)

There are several principles here I don't want you to miss. This fight is bigger than any one person. "Rally to us" is a command to unite together; there's strength in numbers. Let's combine our efforts; let's support one another. The Bible is clear; unity is a strong force and a powerful weapon.

Did you notice that the enemy recognized who guarded, defended, and kept the Israelites safe and empowered them to bounce back? Did you notice that they all went back to work? The wall was not yet completed and now was not the time to take a break. Knowing that God was their guardian empowered them to stay single-minded and determined.

So we may boldly say: "The Lord is my helper; I will not fear. What can man do to me?" (Heb. 13:6)

"For the eyes of the Lord are on the righteous, and His ears are open to their prayers; but the face of the Lord is against those who do evil." And who is he who will harm you if you become followers of what is good? (1 Pet. 3:12-13)

Who is your source? Who promised never to leave you or forsake you? Who promised to go before you and make every crooked path straight? Who told you that the battle is not yours but His? Who told you to stand still and see the salvation of the Lord? David declared—

The Lord is my light and my salvation; whom shall I fear? The Lord is the strength of my life; of whom shall I be afraid? When the wicked came against me to eat up my flesh, my enemies and foes, they stumbled and fell. Though an army may encamp against me, my heart shall not fear; though war may rise against me, in this I will be confident. (Ps. 27:1-3)

TOO FOCUSED TO STOP

Now it happened when Sanballat, Tobiah, Geshem the Arab, and the rest of our enemies heard that I had rebuilt the wall, and that there were no breaks left in it (though at that time I had not hung the doors in the gates), that Sanballat and

Geshem sent to me, saying, "Come, let us meet together among the villages in the plain of Ono." But they thought to do me harm. So I sent messengers to them, saying, "I am doing a great work, so that I cannot come down. Why should the work cease while I leave it and go down to you?" But they sent me this message four times, and I answered them in the same manner. (Neh. 6:1-4)

They were all trying to frighten us, thinking, "Their hands will get too weak for the work, and it will not be completed." [But I prayed,] "Now strengthen my hands. (Neh. 6:9 NIV 1984)

Nehemiah understood the weapon of prayer, not just praying one time—he did that before he ever got started—but continuing to pray in the midst of criticism, weariness, obstacles, and threats. This was a focused prayer—"Strengthen my hands." His first response was not to retaliate or take on a defeated mentality. Nehemiah understood that God was in charge and he cried out to the Source of his strength and the Strength of his life—"Strengthen my hands."

How do you rise above the plots and tricks of the enemy? How do you stand flat-footed and stay determined four times—"But they sent me this message four times, and I answered them in the same manner." What causes a man to persevere under the pressure of defeat?

How you respond to the ploys of the enemy can determine your outcome. Distractions can come from what we hear. What you hear and meditate on will manifest into actions. What you hear influences how you think, and what you think will influence your actions. Nehemiah knew he could not afford to entertain the negative, insulting, spiteful, and divisive messages that were being sent to him continually.

Sanballat, Tobiah, and Geshem did not stop taunting them. Regardless of how strong we are in the Lord, we must protect our spirit. The enemy is always hoping that we will respond in a carnal way, which would negatively impact our Christian testimony and damage our ability to be a creditable witness. Nehemiah stayed focused in the midst of three separate attacks: (1) personal letters written to bully him, (2) a public letter written to challenge his character, and (3) a warning designed to terrorize him.

The heart of the righteous studies how to answer, but the mouth of the wicked pours forth evil. The Lord is far from the wicked, but He hears the prayer of the righteous. (Prov. 15:28-29)

For we do not wrestle against flesh and blood, but against principalities, against powers, against the rulers of the darkness of this age, against spiritual hosts of wickedness in the heavenly places. (Eph. 6:12-13)

FINISHING STRONG

Leadership is not for wimps. Nehemiah was a determined leader who was able to influence, impact, and rally his followers to finish strong. The opposition was counting on Nehemiah to become disappointed, discouraged, and disillusioned.

So the wall was completed on the twenty-fifth of Elul, in fifty-two days. When all our enemies heard about this, all the surrounding nations were afraid and lost their self-confidence, BECAUSE THEY REALIZED THAT THIS WORK HAD BEEN DONE WITH THE HELP OF OUR GOD. (Neh. 6:15-16)

Confusion, fear, and doubt are emotions the enemy uses to keep you off balance. Embrace the ten steps below and you too will go from vision to victory.

- Identify the areas of your life that lay ruined.
- Establish a praying relationship with God.
- Assess where you are and where you should be, based upon your potential.

- Become uncomfortable and lament over your present situation.
- Acknowledge your sins and cry out to God for deliverance.
- Have the courage to start where you are.
- Choose carefully your support team.
- Expect resistance and opposition from the devil.
- Don't quit or throw in the towel.
- Stay single-minded, determined, and purpose-driven.

TESTIMONY: MONICA ST. LOUIS
The Birth of a Promise

On February 15, 2013, I knew that I had to officially go through with the divorce and close that chapter of my life. When 2014 came around, I felt in my spirit that it was time for me to move forward, so I started praying, asking God, what's next? I felt in my spirit that is was time to relocate and start my own business. I had always wanted to own a restaurant; I'd been talking to God about owning one since 2006. (God is never late, but He's always on time.)

I began to pray for direction, because I was not completely sure about the route I should take. Soon after God directed me to attend culinary school (Le Cordon Bleu) for a year. I finished culinary school in the beginning of 2016, and did some temporary restaurant jobs, but I knew that was part of my training. Shortly before we moved, I was in devotion and the Lord confirmed to me that I would have my own restaurant. A name came to mind, as did the slogan and the number of restaurants that I would be blessed with. The following week I got some shirts printed with the restaurant name, and started praying over them; hence the birth of my restaurant blessings. That spring I knew it was time for my relocation, so I started my search for a home in Atlanta.

At one point I started questioning God because it seemed as if nothing was coming through for me. I couldn't find a home within my budget, but even then, I still knew that I was on the right track, so although it was hard, I kept pushing, praying, and believing. I will never forget, while I was cooking breakfast one Sunday morning, the Lord impressed on my heart to start packing. He told me with such a stern voice that I had to immediately buy moving boxes and pack up all my belongings. Still I had my doubts because we didn't have any homes pending and didn't know where we were going to live. We lived out of boxes for the next month before the Lord opened a door for us.

We moved to Atlanta that summer completely on faith. I had no job and I brought my daughters from a place that they were used to to a place that may or may not be promising. *Still*, I trusted God to make a way and to bring us to places we'd never imagined. The home that my ex-husband and I shared was up for sale and I got half of the proceeds. During that time I was diligently seeking a restaurant job. I did not get hired until that October at a catering company; however, I knew there was a bigger mission to be fulfilled.

God did not bring me to another state to have me stay in the same mediocre position. I began to pray about the business and how it would be financed. The Lord started putting people in my path to help me. I contemplated the financing aspects and considered investors and loans. However, the Lord laid it on my heart to use the proceeds from the house sale to start the process. In no time we found a building in a prime location. By December I was able to sign the lease, and God gave me favor with the landlord, so he gave me five months' rent free.

I had some idea of running a restaurant due to the training and experience I had. However, I knew that there was more to it than that, but it was the conversations that I was having with the Lord that kept me going. "Lord, I need help!" I cried, and He sent it. I was introduced to a consulting firm that does start up restaurants, where I received a blueprint of every step, from the realtor, to the architect, to the contractor.

I also did some basic work like register the business name, get tax IDs, and open a bank account. Then the nightmares began. What should have taken six months turned into nine months. It started with the architect. The drawing layouts were being rejected by the county. They kept making changes, but nothing was resolved. I began calling the county. I called and called, and called. I got so frustrated that I went to the county office and sat down with the inspector to get to the bottom of the problem. I also spoke with his supervisor. That day we got it resolved, and were able to get the permit to start the construction. Prior to that I met with the contractor and he gave me a price on the work that needed to be done. I gave him a deposit, and he said work would start immediately and that was a lie! He also said he could have the work done in three months. That too was a lie. We missed two opening dates. His work was slow, sloppy, and unprofessional.

Through the nine months of construction, I dealt with lies, thieves, brick walls, and stagnancy. It did not stop. I had back-to-back new problems. I became tired and angry. I had to say "Lord, what's going on? If this was not what you wanted me to do, then why did you allow me to invest my money in this?" By that time I had already invested around $35,000. But deep down in my heart, I knew I was doing the right thing, and that God had my back, but I had to fight for what was mine. No matter the setbacks I continued pushing forward. I refused to look back. Basically, I couldn't just talk faith—I had to walk it too.

Even through the struggle God started sending the right people my way, whether it was for wholesale on items down to the guys to mount my televisions. It didn't seem things were moving fast enough for me, but it was getting done in God's timing. He was teaching me to "trust in the Lord and lean not unto my own understanding."

After three delayed opening days, we finally opened the doors on October 9, 2017. I'm currently working thirteen plus hours a day. I cook, and do dishes and floors, but I do it with joy. Our God is faithful and my work is not yet done. I know that God has more in store for me to do.

For those who are reading my testimony, stay the course, no matter how hard it gets. Believe God and believe in yourself. He will not call you to do something that He has not already equipped you to do; the calling is inside of you waiting to be birthed. The vision sometimes may tarry for a while, but that doesn't mean you should give up.

Even when you come to a standstill, you are backed into a corner, and God is not answering any of your prayers, don't give up. That's when frustration comes in, and the enemy wants you to walk away, or give up, but don't you dare. God knows why things happen and He is watching to see if you are going to listen to Him or walk away. God is faithful and He also has His own time schedule. Remember, He doesn't go with our schedule; we're called to go with His.

CHAPTER 10
THIS IS A PERSONAL FIGHT
(Rebound and Recover)

This is a war cry: "The Lord goes out to fight like a warrior; he is ready and eager for battle. He gives a war cry, a battle shout; he shows his power against his enemies." (Isa. 42:13 TEV)

YOUR ABILITY TO FIGHT AND WIN is often based upon how you see your situation. You are too strong to let the devil kill you. You've been through too much to let the devil destroy you. You've sacrificed too much to let the devil rob you. It doesn't matter how long you've been standing; now is not the time to throw in the towel. I don't care how bad it hurts; you must keep your faith. I don't care what you have to do to get up every day; keep your faith. The devil has a strategic plan in every situation. This is not the time to die, not the time to give up, and not the time to go backward.

Sometimes the closest people to you will not be there to support you. You must be able to encourage yourself when you're alone and there is no praise team or choir to lead you into the presence of God. When you call the cell phone of everyone you know and no one answers and no one calls you back, you must know how to get your second wind. If you're going to recover all, you're going to have to pick yourself up, get your act together, talk faith to yourself, quote Scripture to yourself, and sing at the top of your lungs, even if you can't hold a note. Leave yourself a voicemail and write yourself an email declaring—

I will bless the Lord at all times: his praise shall continually be in my mouth. My soul shall make her boast in the Lord: the humble shall hear thereof, and be glad. O magnify the Lord with me, and let us exalt his name together. (Ps. 34:1-3 KJV)

The problem is, there is no "let us exalt his name together." It's only you and it's imperative that you learn how to go from the Outer Court into the Holy of Holies for yourself and by yourself.

The story of David at Ziklag underscores the importance of being able to challenge yourself to persevere, when no one else is building you up and there are some who are waiting to see you defeated. Saul had driven David from his country, the Philistines had driven him from their camp, and the Amalekites had plundered his city, and taken the women and children as prisoners.

Now it happened, when David and his men came to Ziklag, on the third day, that the Amalekites had invaded the South and Ziklag, attacked Ziklag and burned it with fire, and had taken captive the women and those who were there, from small to great; they did not kill anyone, but carried them away and went their way. So David and his men came to the city, and there it was, burned with fire; and their wives, their sons, and their daughters had been taken captive. Then David and the people who were with him lifted up their voices and wept, until they had no more power to weep. And David's two wives, Ahinoam the Jezreelitess, and Abigail the widow of Nabal the Carmelite, had been taken captive. (1 Sam. 30:1-5 NKJV)

David and six hundred men had fought many battles and had never lost one. They were returning home from a battle, only to find that the village has been destroyed. As they approached their city, they could see the smoke, but they had no idea that the city had been burned, their wealth had been seized, and their wives and children had been kidnapped by the Amalekites, one of the enemies of the Israelites. The attack denotes three areas of our lives that the enemy attacks: (1) our possessions, (2) our relationships (covenant), and (3) our future (children).

Now David was greatly distressed, for the people spoke of stoning him, because the soul of all the people was grieved, every man for his sons and his daughters. But David strengthened himself in the Lord his God. (1 Sam. 30:6 NKJV)

No two people respond the same way to the same circumstances; even believers react differently based upon their level of faith in the Word of God. The men who wanted to stone David obviously were not thinking rationally. Grief, sorrow, and despair overwhelmed them and instead of supporting their leader, there were those who allowed their pain to cloud their perspective. David's two wives and family had also been abducted and he was "greatly distressed," and in anguish; however, as the leader, it was his responsibility to rally the men.

One three-letter word made all the difference: "but"—"But David strengthened himself in the Lord his God." On one hand David was dealing with calamities, loss, treachery, and peril; and on the other hand, trust and dependency on God. I want to share with you four keys to recovering what the enemy has stolen from you.

REMEMBER THAT GOD IS THE SOURCE OF YOUR STRENGTH.

While that may appear to be elementary, it blows my mind how many believers fall to pieces and crumble under the weight of trying to survive on their own. Stop trying to find reassurance and reinforcement from your family, your friendships, your co-workers, and even your enemies. Notice that David's confidence was based upon his relationship with his covenant-keeping God. Too many believers base their faith on the testimony of someone else who has a track record and a relationship with God.

This is what the Word of God declares—

So we may boldly say: "The Lord is my helper; I will not fear. What can man do to me?" (Heb. 13:6 NKJV)

But those who wait on the Lord shall renew their strength; they shall mount up with wings like eagles, they shall run and not be weary, they shall walk and not faint. (Isa. 40:31 NKJV)

I can do all things through Christ who strengthens me. (Phil. 4:13 NKJV)

I will lift up my eyes to the hills—From whence comes my help? My help comes from the Lord, Who made heaven and earth. (Ps. 121:1 NKJV)

SEEK GOD FOR DIRECTION.

Proverbs 3:5-6 declares, "Trust in the Lord with all your heart, and lean not on your own understanding; in all your ways acknowledge Him, and He shall direct your paths." This is why David had to get a grip on his emotions. He had to focus on God's answer, not the problem. When emotions are driving our decisions, we tend to make bad choices. David had to be levelheaded, intentional, and strategic.

So David inquired of the Lord, saying, "Shall I pursue this troop? Shall I overtake them?" And He answered him, "Pursue, for you shall surely overtake them and without fail recover all." (1 Sam. 30:8 NKJV)

Take note that David was not expecting God to help him without him doing his part to engage the enemy and fight for what belonged to him. "Shall I pursue" (chase, hunt, capture, engage, go for it) does not translate into "wait, postpone, put off, delay, linger." Now don't overlook the fact that God quickly responded to David's prayer. There are too many Scriptures that reinforce the fact that we are in relationship with our Heavenly Father who wants to be actively involved in the affairs of our lives—

In my distress I called upon the Lord, and cried out to my God; He heard my voice from His temple, and my cry came before Him, even to His ears. (Ps. 18:6 NKJV)

It shall come to pass that before they call, I will answer; and while they are still speaking, I will hear. (Isa. 65:24 NKJV)

He shall call upon Me, and I will answer him; I will be with him in trouble; I will deliver him and honor him. (Ps. 91:15 NKJV)

"Call to Me, and I will answer you, and show you great and mighty things, which you do not know." (Jer. 33:3 NKJV)

NEVER BE INTIMIDATED BY THE ENEMY

Once David was assured that he was in the will of God and victory was inevitable (this was a fight of his faith), he wasn't doubleminded, he didn't vacillate, nor did he procrastinate. Too often we're not prepared to fight and we don't have the spiritual foundation to endure.

So David went, he and the six hundred men who were with him, and came to the Brook Besor, where those stayed who were left behind. But David pursued, he and four hundred men; for two hundred stayed behind, who were so weary that they could not cross the Brook Besor. (1 Sam. 30:9-10 NKJV)

David didn't send his men to war. He went himself and took with him all the forces he had, but a third of his men were so fatigued and drained from their anguish and sorrow, that they could not make the journey and cross over the brook. This was a defining moment for David. He was basing his victory on the word of God, but he was counting on his men of war to accomplish the defeat of the Amalekites. How often do we become anxious, when our circumstances look contrary to what God has promised and our faith is challenged to stay the course despite what we see, hear, and feel? David did not waver in his resolve to pursue the enemy. He never forced the two hundred stragglers to change their minds; he didn't belittle them, nor did he reject them.

COUNT THE COST AND BE PREPARED TO FIGHT

Then David attacked them from twilight until the evening of the next day. Not a man of them escaped, except four hundred young men who rode on camels and fled. (1 Sam. 30:17 NKJV)

Even though victory was guaranteed, who knows whether they were prepared to fight for over twenty-four hours? The Amalekites had been drinking and were celebrating their great victory when David and his men attacked and caught the camp by the element of surprise. They killed all the Amalekites, except four hundred young men who escaped, rescued all the people who had been kidnapped, and recovered all their belongings.

So David recovered all that the Amalekites had carried away, and David rescued his two wives. And nothing of theirs was lacking, either small or great, sons or daughters, spoil or anything which they had taken from them; David recovered all. (1 Sam. 30:18-19 NKJV)

Even though they were greatly outnumbered, God empowered them to fight long and hard and they recovered all of their family members and more possessions than they had ever had before.

And that about wraps it up. God is strong, and he wants you strong. So take everything the Master has set out for you, well-made weapons of the best materials. And put them to use so you will be able to stand up to everything the Devil throws your way. This is no afternoon athletic contest that we'll walk away from and forget about in a couple of hours. This is for keeps, a life-or-death fight to the finish against the Devil and all his angels. Be prepared. You're up against far more than you can handle on your own. Take all the help you can get, every weapon God has issued, so that when it's all over but the shouting you'll still be on your feet. (Eph. 6:10-14 MSG)

You are at a crossroad today and you have three choices. Number one, you can live in reverse, lamenting over the mistakes of the past, the decisions you made that have you where you are today, or your choices that have negatively impacted your life. Number two, you can assume a victim mentality and remain in your present situation with no peace, no joy, and no vision of a preferred future because the enemy has clouded your perspective. I hope I'm painting a picture that is causing something in you to get uncomfortable and move you from complacency to change.

Your final choice is to rebound and recover. You can recover because it's not too late. Your financial situation can be turned around; it's not too late. You can recover from a tragedy or a mistake; it's not too late. You can stop living beneath your privileges; it's not too late. You can change the way you see yourself; it's not too late. You can forgive the person who hurt you; it's not too late. You can surrender your life to Jesus; it is definitely not too late.

TESTIMONY: MIN. INEZ W. BUSH
Learning How to Suffer in the Safe Place

God gave me 1 Peter 4 while I was in the middle of the worst part of my storm.

At the age of sixteen, I was diagnosed with cervical cancer. My mom would not allow for me to have a complete hysterectomy and thanks be to God she didn't. But at that time they

I COMMAND YOU TO FIGHT

froze my cervix. After many years of complications and much pain, I gave birth to a baby boy on February 16, 1986. After he was born, they had to do several procedures to stop me from hemorrhaging. Then I gave birth to my second son on September 10, 1988. He was only two weeks old when they discovered that the cancer had returned in my ovaries.

At that time, they did a complete hysterectomy. I was only twenty-one years old. Married with two small children, within the same year I had to have surgery again on my bladder. The cancer had invaded the wall of my bladder. Then when my youngest son was approximately two years old, I had six surgeries in one year. The cancer went from the cervix to the ovaries to the bladder to my left kidney to my colon. Finally, they did a bone marrow scan and discovered that I had a plastic anemia. Chemotherapy and radiation affected my heart, so in September of 2001 I had to have an ablation done on my heart. Thanks be to God I was already in the hospital suffering with a pain crisis due to the fact that I have sickle cell anemia as well.

On this day I woke up to my heart beating 212 beats a minute. The doctors were *amazed*. Needless to say, they rushed me to surgery immediately. And later informed me that I was a miracle. Then later in 2003 due to a problem with my port, I had a blood clot that went undetected for some time but thanks be to God again I was in the hospital having one of the surgeries on my colon when they discovered the blood clot had gone to my brain. I don't remember much about this time. I just remember them calling my family to inform them that I probably would not make it. But God. I had limited sight for five to seven days and oh what a celebration when I walked out of the hospital. I still have many struggles, but I recognize if God brought me through all that, He can truly do the impossible.

How did you handle it? In the beginning I was a very scared little girl. I had no idea what was happening to me. I thought every woman experienced bleeding and pain the way I did. I have always had a very close and personal relationship with

God. I have been playing the piano and directing choirs since I was twelve years old. So I would listen to the lyrics of the songs that I would teach, and I literally took God at His word. The hardest part of going through so much at a young age was feeling so alone. Although I had many people around who loved and cared for me. The one person I needed and wanted the most was my ex-husband, the father of my children. He left and we divorced. I tried to commit suicide but God had another plan. Basically I had to learn to totally trust God. In 1999, God allowed me to write and produce a CD and that helped me to verbalize my gratitude to God.

What did you do to fight? This one is pretty simple. Every morning when I would wake up and see my two precious children, I knew I had to fight. I knew that nobody could love them the way I could. So I just kept putting one foot in front of the other and kept it moving.

How was your faith challenged? It was mostly challenged by church people. Because I was the worship leader/minister of music, people would often question why God would allow me to go through so much. That used to offend me but in the end it made me strong. I just kept studying to show myself approved. A workman need not be ashamed but rightly divide the word of truth. If God allowed Job, Paul, Jonah, and others to go through what they went through, I wasn't any better than they were. So that helped to increase my faith.

What was the outcome? I presently still struggle with many issues due to what has happened. They say that I will never be cancer free but I believe God and as I said, I just keep putting one foot in front of the other.

How are you different today? I thank God every day for trusting me to bear this cross. I know that I am healed and I am VICTORIOUS.

*Special note: My oldest son suffers with many mental diagnoses and has been in and out of jail since the age of seventeen.

I believe my son had a hard time watching his mother and little brother suffer so much. The baby boy suffers from sickle cell anemia SS. He has had two strokes and many hospital stays. He and I both have been in and out of hospice. Like I said, but God.

After about the sixth surgery on my colon, I had to wear a colostomy bag for a while. During this time I had a staph infection so I could not leave the hospital; I was in Crawford Long Hospital for three months. They then did the reconstructive surgery and removed the bag and reconnected what was left of my intestines. I have a plastic piece that I have to have adjusted every so often (I know when it's time because it becomes painful and uncomfortable). I also have to have my esophagus stretched every so often as well. These things are due to my treatments over the years. After having over forty major operations, my muscles in my stomach became very weak which in turned caused several hiatal hernia which I've also had to have surgery on. My total amount of surgeries are forty-five: three on my heart, three on my ankle from a bad car accident (my bones don't heal properly due to my diagnosis), and the remainder of them from cancer. My son could go on and on. I was in tears listening to what he remembers as a child being sick himself! Darren, my baby boy, has been on life support twice and has had two strokes, but shared with me the worst pain he has ever felt was watching me go through all my health struggles.

I have been through BUT he told me that's how he learned to fight. To God be the glory for every trial we've gone through because it made us strong. I don't want to leave my oldest son out of this testimony. He is one anointed young man but turned to drugs, the streets, and whatever he could get his hands on to numb the pain he was in, having to watch his brother and I suffer. Eventually he ended up in jail and in mental hospitals. I love my children, but it has been a real struggle with one being physically sick and the other mentally ill. Yet God has proven to me and my family He is yet faithful.

CHAPTER II
SURVIVING AN ATTACK
(Refuse to Retreat)

F ROM GENESIS TO REVELATION, the Bible is clear: we have an enemy, we are in a war, and the objective is our defeat and destruction (John 10:10). It is paramount for believers to be able to identify the adversary, recognize an attack, and comprehend the tactics of our enemy—

For we do not wrestle against flesh and blood, but against principalities, against powers, against the rulers of the darkness of this age, against spiritual hosts of wickedness in the heavenly places. (Eph. 6:12 NKJV)

I Command You to Fight is for every believer who understands that you have a mandate, a commission from God to know your enemy. Jesus exposed the lies the enemy has successfully perpetrated against us. Keep in mind that spirits seek human vessels to accomplish their assignments. Our responsibility is to identify the spirit that is operating through an individual and maintain a position of power through the Holy Spirit. We have been empowered with knowledge (to know what to do), wisdom (to know how to apply knowledge), and authority to destroy the works of the devil.

The Apostle Paul warned the church at Corinth that if we do not comprehend how our enemy operates, he will take advantage of us—"Lest Satan should take advantage of us; for we are not ignorant of his devices" (2 Cor. 2:11 NKJV). "Ignorance" is defined as "lacking in knowledge." Our ignorance benefits the devil because it is impossible to fight in a battle and win against an opponent you have not identified or do not understand his method of operation.

When God delivered Moses and the children of Israel from the grips of Pharaoh, that was a breakthrough, the beginning of a new way of life. What you must understand is, that was round one of the fight. The spirit of fear, intimidation, and hatred overshadowed Pharaoh and he changed his mind, and mounted an attack against the Israelites with a vengeance.

As believers we know that Jesus has already defeated death, the grave, and hell, but nowhere does Scripture teach that the new birth automatically eliminates demonic attacks in our lives. Even Jesus had to deal with the attacks of Satan. Satan strategically planned an attack after Jesus' baptism and the affirmation by God, that He was His Son. Now Satan knew whom to attack and immediately he looked for an opportunity to destroy Him. Satan didn't back down and he wasn't intimidated. Picture Jesus in a four-round boxing match with the devil.

Round #1: Do you know who you are?

Satan knew that Jesus had come to bring salvation, and he knew that if he could get Jesus to sin, that would ruin the whole plan of salvation. "For this purpose the Son of God was manifested, that He might destroy the works of the devil" (1 John 3:8 NKJV).

Round #2: Will you operate independently from God to meet your needs?

Satan was tempting Christ to act independently of the Holy Spirit, who had led him into the wilderness. He was seeking to destroy the Son's confidence in His Father's will and power to sustain Him. Satan is always trying to get believers to doubt God.

Round #3: Will you detour from your destiny to fulfill your own agenda?

Satan was tempting Him by saying, "So you trust your Father? Let's see how much you trust God. If you will not work a miracle for yourself, then let God work one for you and since you seem to know Scripture, let me give you one," and he proceeded to quote from Psalm 91—"For He shall give His angels charge over you, to keep you in all your ways. In their hands they shall bear you up, lest you dash your foot against a stone" (Ps. 91:11-12 NKJV).

However, Satan twisted the Word, hoping that Jesus would distrust and the Messiah would fall upon the rocks and die. This would end God's plan of salvation.

Round #4: Will you test the grace and mercy of God?

Satan knows that everyone likes power, so he offers Christ position and prestige. He knows that Jesus was promised the kingdom, but he offered Jesus a shortcut to His kingdom. Jesus knew that the kingdom was His after suffering and dying on the cross. He could have the kingdom now if He would only bow down and worship Satan just once. Remember, Satan's goal has always been to take the place of God.

Now, I'm writing to someone who is under attack right now. You lost a round, but you haven't lost the fight. The enemy fights those who know who they are. God is with you, God is for you, and God is more than the world (and every demon of hell) against you. Jesus taught that "the kingdom suffers violence" and violent men take it by force (Matt. 11:12). The violence of the Kingdom is not physical violence but a relentless pursuit to never give up or throw in the towel.

At the end of Jesus' forty days of fasting and praying in the wilderness, He was physically weak and mentally drained, but spiritually, Jesus came forth with an anointing to destroy the works of the evil one—"Then Jesus returned in the power of the Spirit to Galilee" (Luke 4:14 NKJV).

There is no record that the children of Israel ever had to fight any battles in Egypt, but once they were delivered from bondage, they discovered they had enemies. In Egypt they were slaves, prisoners under the ruthless Pharaoh, who feared that if they continued to multiply, they would be a security risk and one day side with his enemies. To the Egyptians' dismay, the children of Israel grew stronger under Egyptian brutality.

But the children of Israel were fruitful and increased abundantly, multiplied and grew exceedingly mighty; and the land was filled with them. Now there arose a new king over Egypt, who did not know Joseph. And he said to his people, "Look, the people of the children of Israel are more and mightier than we; come, let us deal shrewdly with them, lest they multiply, and it happen, in the event of war, that they also join our enemies and fight against us, and so go up out of the land." Therefore they set taskmasters over them to afflict them with their burdens. And they built for Pharaoh supply cities, Pithom and Raamses. But the more they afflicted them, the more they multiplied and grew. And they were in dread of the children of Israel. (Exod. 1:7-12 NKJV)

Frustration turned into manslaughter and all Jewish boys were given a death sentence. Midwives were instructed to kill Hebrew baby boys and eventually drown them to ensure that they would not be able to reproduce, but one baby boy was born whom Pharaoh couldn't kill. God's plan was for Moses to be the instrument of their deliverance from slavery.

I Command You to Fight is not just a book of biblical stories. What does God want us to learn from what we've read? Number one, what the enemy uses to try to destroy you, God will use to strengthen you to overcome. Number two, your purpose and assignment were settled before you were even born. When you walk in it, you become a threat to the kingdom of darkness.

Even on the night of their deliverance from Egypt, the children of Israel had to fight fear and panic as Pharaoh and his Egyptian army chased them with a vengeance. God revealed himself as their rear guard and fought for them—

And Moses said to the people, "Do not be afraid. Stand still, and see the salvation of the Lord, which He will accomplish for you today. For the Egyptians whom you see today, you shall see again no more forever. The Lord will fight for you, and you shall hold your peace." (Exod. 14:13-14 NKJV)

Fast forward and we now find Moses and the children of Israel as nomads, free from bondage and journeying toward their Promised Land. They were free from slavery, but now they have new enemies. Esau opposed his brother Jacob and threatened to kill him (Gen. 27:41), and Esau's descendants, the Amalekites, opposed the children of Jacob (Israel) and threatened to annihilate them.

Now Amalek came and fought with Israel in Rephidim. And Moses said to Joshua, "Choose us some men and go out, fight with Amalek. Tomorrow I will stand on the top of the hill with the rod of God in my hand." So Joshua did as Moses said to him, and fought with Amalek. (Exod. 17:8-10 NKJV)

This is the first mention of Joshua in the Bible. He was born in Egypt and named Hoshea, which means "Jehovah is salvation" (Num. 13:8, 16), and is the Hebrew equivalent of "Jesus" (Matt. 1:21; Heb. 4:8). Moses changed his name to Joshua, placed him in a military position to lead the attack against the Amalekites, and gave him one day to recruit an army to fight.

And Moses, Aaron, and Hur went up to the top of the hill. And so it was, when Moses held up his hand, that Israel prevailed; and when he let down his hand, Amalek prevailed.

But Moses' hands became heavy; so they took a stone and put it under him, and he sat on it. And Aaron and Hur supported his hands, one on one side, and the other on the other side; and his hands were steady until the going down of the sun. (Exod. 17:10-12 NKJV)

It was customary for the Jews to lift up their hands when they prayed (Pss. 28:2; 44:20; 63:4; 134:2; 1 Tim. 2:8). When Moses held up the staff of God, he was confessing total dependence on the authority and power of God. As long as Moses held the rod up, Israel overcame; but when his arms became weak and he dropped them, Amalek prevailed.

While Joshua and his army fought on the front line, Aaron and Hur stood on top of the hill, holding up the arms of their leader, Moses. God could have sent angels to destroy the Amalekites (Isa. 37:36), but he chose to show Himself strong to Israel and their enemies. Israel's victory was secured because of the power of God, the strength of Joshua and the army on the battlefield, and the constant prayers of Moses, Aaron, and Hur, as they interceded on top of the hill.

So Joshua defeated Amalek and his people with the edge of the sword. Then the Lord said to Moses, "Write this for a memorial in the book and recount it in the hearing of Joshua, that I will utterly blot out the remembrance of Amalek from under heaven." And Moses built an altar and called its name, The-Lord-Is-My-Banner; for he said, "Because the Lord has sworn: the Lord will have war with Amalek from generation to generation." (Exod. 17:13-16 NKJV)

Joshua would not have been victorious without Moses and Moses could not have succeeded without the support of Aaron and Hur. In reality it wasn't Moses who was empowering Joshua and his army; it was the God of Abraham, Isaac, and Jacob, "Jehovah Sabaoth" (the Lord of Hosts). So Moses built an altar and named it "Jehovah Nissi" (The Lord is my Banner).

So what can we glean from the defeat of the Amalekites? First, God honors His covenant and He will protect and defend His people. Second, God has not called everyone to be a Moses or Joshua, but every believer needs to know how to fight, how to stand in support, and how to go before God in prayer (Rom. 12:12; Isa. 59:16). Third, true intercession is not for wimps. It's a call that requires spiritual muscles and the ability to "pray without ceasing" (1 Thess. 5:17).

Fourth, I want you to look at where Aaron and Hur were positioned. They were not in the forefront, in the midst of the battle, where everyone could see them. They were in the shadows, with one assignment, to lift up the arms of their leader. Aaron was a priest, who could have gotten in the flesh and determined he was too anointed to humble himself to lift up his brother's arms. Hur was a leader who easily could have said, "You could have chosen me instead of Joshua." What's the takeaway? Don't ever think more highly of yourself, be faithful over small assignments, and watch how God will open doors for you. Every failure is a prayer failure and without prayer (intercession), we cannot survive an attack. In addition, we don't know how long Joshua and the men had to fight. When we pray for "strength in your inner man," God's supernatural grace empowers you to stand.

The fifth lesson we need to remember is that we have the presence of the Holy Spirit to intercede for us and lead us into all truth (Rom. 8:26-27). Our final takeaway is a reminder that Jesus sits at the right hand of the Father, daily interceding for us.

Moses understood that a battle and the war were two separate events. Long after he was dead, he wanted the Israelites to remember that they had an enemy who needed to be destroyed or they would forever be under attack. In the official book of records, he instructed Israel to contend with Amalek until that nation was completely destroyed. Israel fought them again at Kadesh-Barnea but they were defeated—

Then the Amalekites and the Canaanites who dwelt in that mountain came down and attacked them, and drove them back as far as Hormah (Num. 14:45 NKJV).

In the Book of Deuteronomy, Moses rehearses the history and future promises of God. In the twenty-fifth chapter of Deuteronomy, Moses describes the strategy of the Amalekites.

"Remember what Amalek did to you on the way as you were coming out of Egypt, how he met you on the way and attacked your rear ranks, all the stragglers at your rear, when you were tired and weary; and he did not fear God. Therefore it shall be, when the Lord your God has given you rest from your enemies all around, in the land which the Lord your God is giving you to possess as an inheritance, that you will blot out the remembrance of Amalek from under heaven. You shall not forget." (Deut. 25:17-19 NKJV)

The Israelites were on a celebratory high, singing and dancing, when water came out of the rocks and they were able to drink. The strategy of the enemy was to attack when they least expected it.

"Remember what Amalek did to you on the way as you were coming out of Egypt, how he met you on the way and attacked your rear ranks ..." (Deut. 25:17-18 NKJV)

It was a sneak attack from behind. The attack was designed to stop their progress. The attack was designed to systemically eliminate them.

The enemy attacked the stragglers, those who couldn't keep up, individuals who were weak, exhausted, and ready to faint. They attacked the people who were on the verge of giving up and throwing in the towel—"All the stragglers at your rear, when you were tired and weary" (Deut. 25:18 NKJV). It is one thing for the enemy not to be afraid of the Israelites, but what bothers me the most when I read the Scripture, was the fact that the Amalekites were not afraid of God—"and he did not fear God" (Deut. 25:18 NKJV). When the enemy doesn't fear you or your God, watch out.

What lessons can we learn from Deuteronomy 25? First, the enemy will attack when we least expect it and we are not prepared. Second, the enemy studies each one of us to determine where we are weak. Third, there is safety and protection when we stay connected to our power source and other believers.

There are five distinct times that you can expect spiritual attacks. First, Satan attacks when we go from having a "form of godliness" (2 Tim. 3:5) to being "transformed by the renewing of our minds" (Rom. 12:1-2). Attacks will increase when you: (a) become a worshipper (not just an attender), (b) began to study the Word (not just hear it on Sunday), (c) become a tither (not just an infrequent giver), and (d) become purpose-driven (not just aimlessly living).

Second, attacks may come when you become "salt and light," when your life becomes a living testimony and you become a witness for the Kingdom of God. You go to the top of the hit list and Satan works overtime to discourage you, distract you, and ultimately destroy you.

Third, attacks may come when you uncover and expose Satan for who he is, a "defeated foe." The enemy has intimidated too many believers and convinced them that they cannot overcome him. Paul warns the church at Corinth, "Lest Satan should take advantage of us; for we are not ignorant of his devices" (2 Cor. 2:11 NKJV). When you are determined to advance the Kingdom of God through your level of influence, you will come under attack.

Fourth, attacks will take place when you "die to yourself" and your greatest desire is to live for Him and walk in holiness (not a denomination, but a way of life). The enemy expects your unmet need, unhealed hurts, and unresolved issues to sabotage your ability to break free.

Fifth, attacks happen when you are on the verge of a break-through or a supernatural blessing. The enemy's scheme is to overwhelm you with disappointments, frustrations, and delays, hoping that you will move out of the perfect will of God, abort your assignment, or lower your expectation.

Be aware, be on guard, and never let your present situation dictate how you move forward in God. Years ago I preached a sermon, "Abstinence Is Not Deliverance." There are areas in your life that you have struggled to gain victory over and you have had seasons of success. The enemy is forever looking to see if you are strong enough to maintain your victory. Whatever you did to break free from bondage (prayer, fasting, positive declarations, Bible study, etc.), you must continue to do. You cannot let your guard down and get comfortable and complacent now that you think you've been delivered.

While Gideon was able at one point to conquer the Amalekites along with the Midianites (Judg. 6:33), King Saul failed to obey God and exterminate the Amalekites and as a result he forfeited the kingdom (1 Sam. 15) and was later killed by an Amalekite (2 Sam. 1:1-16). David defeated the Amalekites who raided his camp (1 Sam. 30) and finally subdued them when he became king (2 Sam. 8:11-12).

God allows us to face opposition to strengthen our faith and to build up our character. You can fight one time and be a conqueror, but the Bible says that we are "more than conquerors." You go from being a conqueror to a champion when your mindset is to always win. Some problems come to develop you, others come to defeat you. The enemy comes to overthrow, overtake, and overwhelm you. You are valuable in the plan of God. God warns us throughout the Bible that what we don't defeat will defeat us.

No test or temptation that comes your way is beyond the course of what others have had to face. All you need to remember is that God will never let you down; he'll never let you be pushed past your limit; he'll always be there to help you come through it. (1 Cor. 10:13 MSG)

TESTIMONY: ROBIN LAGROW
"The Marriage Made Me Strong"

The marriage had never really been a good one. We got married without really understanding one another and we were blind to so many things. I truly wish that even one of the many people I served under at the time would have spoken into our lives before we said our vows. I also understand that young folks don't always receive advice, especially not when they think they are in love.

So much of our marriage survived because we were youth leaders at our church. Our lives were consumed by these amazing teenagers who spent almost every weekend at our home. I was in need of affection and the ability to nurture. That was definitely NOT my husband's strength or even his interest. Therefore, I turned to the teens to provide that for me. We had special hugs and handshakes, and little things that, without my knowledge, provided what I wasn't receiving from him. On the other hand, he wasn't about emotion ... not even the slightest amount. So, for him to sit at the kitchen table with some of the teens until all hours of the night into the morning was satisfying his need for companionship. I was thriving on the drama resolution; he was thriving on the recreational companionship.

We just weren't thriving with each other. About nine years into our marriage, I was beginning to respond to the absence of true affection from my husband. I didn't realize at the time that was the problem; I just knew that I had never experienced anxiety attacks before. I wasn't even able to drive my car on the interstate without having massive anxiety attacks. I couldn't sit on the inside of a booth in a restaurant and there was no way I could sit in a drive through that had no access for escape. Everything about that made me feel trapped. I had no idea where this was coming from but to say it made our marriage worse is an understatement.

The fact that he had no capacity to nurture me only made him resent and criticize when I would become emotional. I often heard, "If you think you're going to get my attention from crying, you couldn't be more incorrect." My reaction would be, well, to cry some more. At this point, reality was beginning to surface. We were a broken union.

I would give anything if I would have had the courage in that moment to step up and do something to fix our marriage. But because I knew he would not receive the suggestion that I needed anything from him, my best option, in my opinion, was to suck it up and do my best to make it work. I got on meds for anxiety and began that long road of avoiding the obvious, detouring around the conflict.

On the ten-year anniversary of our marriage, we decided to go to Callaway Gardens for a weekend. In some ways it seems that it would shock me that we did that. But we had gotten pretty good at masking our issues, and applying our personal survival responses to keep things moving along. We had a nice dinner and a not-so-terrible evening together and fell asleep in each other's grasp. I woke up feeling some hope. He woke up and said, "If we're going to ever have a baby, we need to do it pretty soon, don't you think?" To say I was stunned is correct. In the back of my mind I had to know that a baby wasn't going to repair us. But in the front of my mind I heard "We must not be doing so badly after all. He wouldn't want a baby if he was finished with our marriage." All thoughts of needing help were pushed aside. We gave up the youth group and started planning our family. Three quick months later I was pregnant.

We bought some property and built a house. Because it wasn't complete when our lease was up on the apartment, we moved in with some of our best friends. We lived there for six months of the pregnancy, while we completed the house. All through the pregnancy we had the project of the house, the pregnancy, and the presence of our friends to do what we had always done, avoid the truth that our marriage was broken. All of those things provided what we didn't give to each other.

Shortly after our beautiful daughter was born, our problems returned. We were back at it, and it was getting worse. My anxiety built up; his stonewalling increased. I got louder; he got quieter. I pushed forward; he backed away. I opened up; he shut down. You get the picture. This went on through a business partnership dissolving, and our daughter growing so quickly. I knew we were a mess, but it seemed to be a mess we could live with. After all, we'd done so for fifteen years.

In June of our fifteenth year together, I was making breakfast for dinner. He was sitting at the computer, which was about twenty feet away from where I stood flipping pancakes. He casually asked me what I had meant a few weeks earlier when I implied that I was done after we had an argument. I casually replied that I just meant I was finished arguing about the subject we were discussing. His response was, "Well, I'm done." I said that was awesome and that there was no reason to keep arguing about it anyway. He said, "You're not hearing me. I'm done. I'm done with you. I come home every day and I know that I love my daughter but I don't love my wife." Well, happy pancakes to me!

There were only a few words spoken about it, as I left the room. I went into the bedroom and called my best friend. In the midst of my tears I simply said, "He said he's done. Now I can fix it." Sounds like a crazy reaction. And yet, when you've lived with someone non-emotional for fifteen years, it sounds like music to your ears to finally get a confession. At least then you know what you're up against. You know what you can work toward. You also know there's a reason you've been so anxious for years. It all made sense to me.

I immediately went into two modes: action and denial. Action to please him. I made his favorite meals every night. I pushed away everyone who spent time with us in an attempt to show him that he was all that mattered. I pushed myself into a box and lived my life to save my marriage. The denial was to survive the fact that I was angry. How could he be done? I was the one who lived a loveless marriage for fifteen years. How could he be done? I was the one who had to rely on teenagers and friends to give me a hug or to hold my hand. How could he be done?

I knew I had turned my crying into fussing. I had turned my emotions into cold-stone glares. But I was doing so to survive. I was doing so to receive *any sort of reaction* out of him. How could he be done? I deserved to be done before he was. Denial helped me ignore those emotions. The goal had to be to save it. I didn't have time to value myself or to give myself permission to feel anything. I had to save it. I had a daughter. I had a family. I had a house. I had a reputation, a ministry. I had to save it. So I lost myself to save the marriage.

From June to December, I became the perfect wife. No demands, no requests. Sex without question. Favorite meals. Gifts. His movie choice. His TV choice. His entertainment choice. I did anything I could do to eliminate stress in his life. Riding down the road, we came up to a traffic signal. For whatever reason, I felt confident to ask a question so I turned to him and said, "We're doing better, aren't we?" I sat there so comfortably knowing I was going to get a great answer. Instead I heard, "I don't know why you're asking me that. Nothing has changed. I still have zero feelings for you."

From that point, I began to unravel. I went to my pastor, who is also my boss and brother. I told him that I needed help and not just the kind where he pulls me into his office and makes it all better. I needed counseling. I needed real help. He connected me with the most amazing person God ever created. This lady eventually became a friend I will treasure for my lifetime.

She was forthright and professional. But she was also real and compassionate. She was a Godsend. She never charged me a dime for counseling. She said the Lord told her not to. Instead she listened to me pour my heart out on a weekly basis. She said to me, "Your marriage may be okay or it may not. But you *will* be okay." It doesn't sound that profound. But to me it was the music of hope being located.

By June of our sixteenth anniversary, he asked if a friend of ours would allow me and our daughter to live with her. That was my exit invitation. Unfortunately, I had no choice but to RSVP. Jordan and I moved in with a friend for four months, and then moved into our own apartment. A year later, we bought a house with my father.

When I had begun counseling, my counselor helped me realize that I was not valuing myself at all. I learned how to remain biblically submissive, but not at the expense of devaluing myself. I learned to see myself as the daughter of the Most High God and I began to treat myself the way my Lord would want me to treat myself. My husband's response to that was, "You sure have gotten mean since you started counseling." My answer: "No, I just now know that I don't deserve to be treated this way." I stopped allowing him to call me names, suggest that I was disgusting, and to go days without speaking to me. I began to stand up for myself. How sad to think that valuing myself was misconstrued by him as being mean.

I knew I would be judged for the divorce. I had a choice to make. I was either going to be judged for being a bitter, man-bashing woman; or I would be judged for being happy. I chose the latter. I decided to not waste another minute of my life fighting this man. I had spent sixteen years of my life fighting with him, for him, against him, to save him. It was finally my turn to control the anxiety, the stress, and the drama.

I chose to forgive. I chose to own it, mourn it, and leave it. I decided to put God, myself, and my daughter in that order of priority. I was broken, but I had hope. I was hurt, but I was loved. I was no longer the pushed aside, ignored, belittled wife. I was the hopeful, free daughter of the King of Kings. I valued my daughter above myself and yet I knew that a healed and whole mom would benefit her more than anything. So I learned to love myself.

By only the grace and love of God, I consider Jordan's dad my friend. It didn't happen overnight. There was much growth required for that to happen, but eventually it did. I lived by 1 Corinthians 14:33— "For God is not a God of disorder but of peace" (NIV).

Today I am a Speaker, a Life Coach, a Coach Trainer, a Pastor, a Mom, and a strong, confident, humble, beautiful, ever-growing, ever-changing Woman! My journey wasn't one of joy, but it was one I've learned from, grown through, and used to empower other women to value themselves enough to make the right decisions for their lives. I wouldn't trade an inch of my journey for anything in the world.

CHAPTER 12
THE CONCLUSION OF THE MATTER
(Stay on the Battlefield)

I Command You to Fight is about overcoming, succeeding, thriving, advancing, and winning. God has given you the land (promises, dreams, desires, rewards), but there are some territories (potential opportunities and promotions) that you are going to have to fight to possess and some (marriage, family, careers, health, prosperity) you will have to battle to keep.

> *"When you go out to battle against your enemies, and see horses and chariots and people more numerous than you, do not be afraid of them; for the Lord your God is with you, who brought you up from the land of Egypt. So it shall be, when you are on the verge of battle that the priest shall approach and speak to the people. And he shall say to them, 'Hear, O Israel: Today you are on the verge of battle with your enemies. Do not let your heart faint, do not be afraid, and do not tremble or be terrified because of them; or the Lord your God is He who goes with you, to fight for you against your enemies, to save you.'"* (Deut. 20:1-4 NKJV)

I COMMAND YOU TO FIGHT

Joshua was given a command to take the children of Israel across the Jordan River into the Promised Land. A land that was theirs to possess, but they would have to fight and dispossess the enemy—

About forty thousand prepared for war crossed over before the Lord for battle, to the plains of Jericho. (Josh. 4:13 NKJV)

Our warfare is spiritual and not against "flesh and blood." We're not in opposition to physical enemies, like people, circumstances, and organizations. We're fighting a hierarchy of demonic forces doing battle in the spiritual realm, but manifesting themselves on earth (Eph. 6:12). We cannot settle for temporary relief; we must destroy the spirits that are coming against us.

One of the greatest weapons we have is the Sword of the Spirit, which is the Word of God. Read it, meditate on it, declare it, and live it. We have been given authority over all the power of the enemy and we are unstoppable. We are vessels of honor and warriors who represent strength and courage.

I Command You to Fight is a reminder to you that you can soar in the midst of chaos, confusion, problems, setbacks, dilemmas, and difficulties. First, recognize your <u>purpose</u> ("I can do all things"); second, recognize your <u>power</u> source ("through Christ"); and third, recognize your <u>potential</u> ("strengthens me") (Phil. 4:13 NKJV).

We must be willing to move forward against all odds. We cannot shrink back or revert back from any challenge. We will be moved, not by might or by power, but by the Spirit of God. (Zech. 4:6)